# Grandma's Fingerprint

# Grandma's Fingerprint

Love a child. Change a life.

## Ann Griffiths

REDEMPTION
PRESS

Published by Redemption Press, PO Box 427, Enumclaw, WA 98022.

Unless otherwise noted, all Scripture verses are taken from *King James Version* of the Bible.

ISBN 13: 978-1-63232-928-8

Library of Congress Catalog Card Number: 2010913350

## Tribute to

—My grandma—
Your life is forever intertwined with mine.

## Dedicated to

—My grandchildren—
For all that you are and all that you will be.

# Contents

# With Gratitude

*Thank you to my husband,* Jim. Your undying love and belief that this book "must be written" spurred me on.

*Thank you to my children,* Sarah and James, and my son-in-law, Sherman Hu. Your unconditional love and consistent words like, "Way to go, Mom," and, "You can do it," never ceased to strengthen my resolve.

*Thank you to my grandchildren,* Victoria, Anthony, Calista, and Lucas. You bless my life every day, more than you ever will know. Your lives are a growing testament of God's faithfulness through generations.

*Thank you to my sister and brothers.* Whether we walk life together or follow our own unique roads, we are family and are there for each other.

*Thank you to my friend and ministry partner,* Donna Inglis. When the writing touched an area of my life that was difficult to face, you stayed right there with me as I worked through to the other side of the struggle.

*Thank you to my editor coach*, Barbara Kois. You believed in me and in the message of this book. Your wisdom, expertise, and dedication to excellence helped me to breathe easier.

# Introduction

W E EACH COME into this world with generations of family history attached to our names. And we each go out of this world having added a chapter or two to our family's legacy.

As I grew from a girl into a young woman, that concept never entered my mind. But when I became a mother, my heritage, and particularly the role that my maternal grandmother played in my life, took on new meaning. Then as I watched my grandma interact with my children, the span of physical years that separated them evaporated, and a timeless connection remained.

Now as a grandma myself, I am overwhelmed at the difference my grandma made in my life. Without her, I would not be the woman I am today. And I realize that my role as a grandma is more important than I ever could imagine.

As you follow the journey that my grandma and I traveled together, it is my hope that if you are a grandma or a grandma-to-be, you will be encouraged in the vital role you play. If you have or have had a grandma, regardless of your relationship with her, may this story of resilience, sorrow, triumph, and loss inspire you to see yourself (and her, if she still is living) as someone who can make a memorable and positive difference in the lives of the next generation.

This book is a tribute to my grandma and a legacy for my family. But it also was written to inspire all grandmas and grandmas-to-be. I did not write it for me; although, it turned out to be a healing salve on the buried wounds that I unknowingly carried, which may be why I wrote a few pages and then threw what I'd written into the closet so many times over the years. It was both one of the most difficult undertakings and one of the most rewarding experiences of my life to date.

*Grandma's Fingerprint* is a story about relationships. It is a story about struggle, triumph, and enduring love. And it is a story that speaks of the faithfulness of God in both the highs and lows of life and the grace of God throughout generations.

## Births, Deaths, Marriages, and Moves

| | | |
|---|---|---|
| 1886 | April 23 | Born: Hurlbert (Bert) Lloyd Imerson (my step-grandpa) in Vancouver, British Columbia, BC |
| 1895 | March 30 | Born: James Kinkaid (my grandpa) in Aberdeen, Scotland |
| 1899 | July 10 | Born: Nancy Mabel Webb (my grandma) in Bishop Storford, Hertfordshire, England |
| 1926 | April 28 | Born: Trevor Patrick Davies Worrall (my dad) |
| 1928 | April 13 | Grandma left England for Canada. |
| 1928 | April 22 | Grandma arrived in Montreal, Quebec, Canada. |

| 1928 | April 28 | Married: Nancy Mabel Webb to James Kinkaid in Stratford, Ontario, Canada |
| 1928 | May 12 | Grandma and Grandpa Kinkaid arrived in Vancouver, BC. |
| | | Lived at 1450 - 36th Avenue East, South Vancouver, BC. |
| 1929 | March | Grandma and Grandpa Kinkaid moved to 1559 - 26th Avenue East, Vancouver, BC. |
| 1929 | November 4 | Born: Doreen Mabel Kinkaid (my mom) in Vancouver, BC |
| 1934 | January 31 | Died: James Kinkaid in Vancouver, BC (my grandpa) |
| 1935 | November 26 | Born: Hurlbert (Herbie) Hoover (Grandpa Imerson's grandson) |
| 1941 | December 3 | Married: Nancy Mabel Webb Kinkaid to Hurlbert (Bert) Lloyd Imerson, in Vancouver, BC |
| 1942 | March 20 | Grandma and Grandpa Imerson and Doreen moved to R.R. 2 Berry Road, Langley Prairie, BC. |
| 1942 | Fall | Herbie came to live with Grandma and Grandpa Imerson. |
| 1944 | January 17 | Grandma and Grandpa Imerson, Doreen, and Herbie moved to Lakeview Farm, Westholme, Vancouver Island, BC. |
| 1944 | August 24 | Grandma and Grandpa, Doreen, and Herbie moved to 1730 Holland Avenue R.R. 3, Victoria, BC. |

| | | |
|---|---|---|
| 1945 | December 15 | Grandma and Grandpa, Doreen, and Herbie moved to 1603 Pacific Highway, R.R. 4, New Westminster, BC (temporary). |
| 1946 | February 19 | Grandma and Grandpa, Doreen, and Herbie moved to 217 Clow and Hjorth Roads R.R. 3, New Westminster, BC. |
| | | The address later changed to 10239 Clow Road, North Surrey, BC. |
| | | The address then changed to 10239 - 156 Street, Surrey, BC. |
| 1946 | December 19 | Born: James (Jim) Reginald Griffiths (my husband-to-be) |
| 1947 | May 12 | Died: Bert Imerson in New Westminster, BC (my step-grandpa) |
| 1949 | January 29 | Married: Doreen Kinkaid to Trevor Worrall (my parents) |
| 1950 | May 2 | Born: Ann Doreen Mabel Worrall (me) |
| 1951 | August 27 | Born: Patricia Flora Lynn Worrall (my sister) |
| 1952 | June 23 | Herbie moved back to Willow River, BC. |
| 1954 | November 20 | Born: Hurlbert (Bert) Trevor Davies Worrall (my brother) |
| 1957 | April 3 | Born: Ian James Worrall (my brother) |
| 1958 | May 9 | Born: Trevor Wesley Peters (my brother) |
| 1959 | May 28 | Born: Keith Roy Thomas Worrall (my brother) |
| 1961 | May 28 | Mom and Dad moved our family from Grandma's. |

| | | |
|---|---|---|
| 1963 | August 16 | Born: Michael Eric Vern Worrall (my brother) |
| 1964 | September 26 | Born: David Arthur William Worrall (my brother) |
| 1971 | June 19 | Married: Ann Worrall to Jim Griffiths in Surrey, BC |
| 1974 | September 22 | Born: Sarah Ann Griffiths (our daughter) |
| 1976 | March 9 | Born: James Samuel Griffiths (our son) |
| 1981 | January 15 | Grandma, Jim, Ann, Sarah, and James moved to 9734 and 9736 - 137A Street, Surrey, BC. |
| 1985 | August 13 | Died: Grandma Imerson at Surrey Memorial Hospital, Surrey, BC |

# CHAPTER 1

# My Dearest Victoria

YOU ARE TOO young to understand what these pages are saying or to imagine why I'm writing them. For now, you're content to sit on my lap in a room filled with family portraits—photos of ancestors I've known and others whose names are mysteries, whose life stories have been lost to the past. We snuggle together as you rest your head on my chest and I stroke your straight, dark hair.

But though you like to be cuddled and loved, you are not one to sit still for long. With in-born curiosity, you point your finger toward the woman in the photo beside us. "Who's that, Grandma?" you ask in your not-quite-three-year-old voice.

"That's your great-great grandma," I reply with pride. "That's Grandma's Grandma."

The photo holds a significant place of honor in our home. It stands alone on a finely polished, wooden end table with a lamp to guide our eyes toward it. No other ornaments or pictures compete for our attention.

As you stare at the photo, a puzzled smile crosses your face, and I see you trying to comprehend what I've said. Then, in typical toddler fashion, you go on to the next question that demands release from your inquisitive mind. For now, our chats are simple—but intimate.

When you are older, our conversations will be more complex. We'll sit together and talk about the deeper questions that your young mind cannot now conceive. And I'll tell you stories that probably will lack detail because of the passing of time. So I'm writing these words while the memories are fresh. I want you to meet the smiling woman in the photo and hear the stories as I remember them today. I want you to feel the warmth of a grandma's love as I share with you the exceptional woman whose life is forever intertwined with mine.

As I look at my grandma's portrait, I realize that for all the memories I have of a "perfect" grandma, she was not perfect. She had knots and imperfections. And though it may be hard for you to imagine that I too have knots and imperfections, don't be disappointed or disillusioned when, one day, you discover them.

Life is much like a tapestry that is knotted and rough on one side and beautiful and clean on the other. There are smooth patches filled with peace and joy. There are rough spots with turmoil and sadness. Life and people are not always what we'd like them to be. Sometimes they fail. Sometimes we fail.

Remember that the knots and flaws are just as important as the joys and accomplishments that we are privileged to experience. Throughout our lives, they all weave us into the individuals we become—unique and beautiful tapestries that God sees as perfect. But it's only as we surrender the knots and imperfections of ourselves and others into the hands of a loving, forgiving, and sovereign God that true brilliance and beauty come alive.

As you read these pages, you'll walk the life journey that my grandma and I traveled together. And though it focuses on the two of us, you'll meet five generations, one of which you are a part.

Each generation adds a different color to the tapestry. Each one leaves a fingerprint on the next generation.

In future years, I will be a portrait on your wall of ancestors. And you will search for words to describe the relationship that you and I, as Grandma and Granddaughter, shared over the years.

May you come to know my grandma and see how her life mingled with mine to help mold me into the grandma I am for you today. May you see the thread of a grandma's unwavering spirit—as it was, as it is, and as it passes from generation to generation to generation. And may you, and others who read this book, be inspired and encouraged by the heart of a grandma's life and love and the difference it made.

One day, when you sit with a child on your lap, may you marvel at what God has done in the lives of those who left a mark on your life. And may the child on your lap be drawn to the beautiful tapestry that is you.

Love,
Grandma

# CHAPTER 2

# The Big Black Car

M Y SIX-YEAR-OLD MIND struggled to make sense of what was happening. *How is Daddy going to know where we went? Will somebody tell him we left in a big black car?*

Dark clouds moved across the sky and covered the last rays of the summer evening sun that reflected against the front of the farmhouse that my father and grandfather had built for my parents when they got married. The two-room house sat on my grandparents' land, across a country road and open field from their English-style cottage and right next to the railroad tracks that ran through the middle of the farm. One room in the house was our living and kitchen area. The second was the bedroom. When our family grew in number, Grandpa and Daddy added another bedroom and a separate kitchen, and the luxury of running water was piped into the small house.

But now we were leaving.

I sat in the back seat of the car, pressed my nose to the side window, and gazed at our silver-gray husky dog as she sat alone in the middle of the yard. Even though Silver was an outside farm dog, my sister and I loved to play with her. In winter, when Daddy harnessed her to the sled, she pulled us around the yard. In summer, she towed us in a wood wagon as we giggled with excitement. Silver was our friend. But now, through my young eyes, our friend looked sad. I wanted to run to her, throw my arms around her thick, furry neck, and tell her we'd be back soon. But would we?

Slowly, the car backed away from our house and onto the road, where it stopped for a moment. Rain began to fall from the gray, cloudy sky. Drops of water bounced off the hood of the car. I could see hollow puffs explode on the ground as the dust that had built up from a long, hot summer welcomed the intrusion.

Stretching as far as I could, I turned and looked out the back window at the neighbor's house, where a light was shining from inside. *Mrs. Bartel will see us leave,* I assured myself. *She sees everything. She'll tell Daddy we left in a big black car.*

Mrs. Bartel spoke with a funny accent, and I was convinced that she was a hundred years old. She was a nice old lady who had goats that provided milk for my sister, who couldn't drink cow's milk. Sometimes Mommy took my sister and me to visit or to sit with Mrs. Bartel's sick husband while she went to the market. When we were in their house, I always smelled old oranges and decided that the oranges must be why Mr. Bartel always was sick.

As the car inched its way over the uneven dirt road, the light from Mr. and Mrs. Bartel's house got smaller and smaller, and I settled down for the ride. Mournful music droned from the car radio while the rain's irregular, pitter-pat-pat rhythm interrupted the steady swoosh-swoosh of the wipers streaking back and forth on the windshield.

My little sister, Patsy, sat next to me in the back seat of the car, her chin flirting with her chest as her head bobbed to the movement of the car. In the front seat, my two-year-old brother, Bertie, already was asleep on Mommy's lap.

While Mommy talked softly to the strange lady driving the big black car, I strained to hear what they were saying.

Earlier, when the lady came to our door, she greeted Mommy like they knew each other, but I hadn't seen her before. She was shorter than Mommy and had dark, curly hair.

"This is Aunt Irene," Mommy had told us.

I knew she wasn't really our aunt, but we had been taught to call all our parents' friends "aunt" or "uncle." There were no exceptions—even if we didn't like them.

My tired body wrestled between sleep and curiosity—not wanting to miss a word that was being said in the front seat. I wondered why Aunt Irene seemed impatient and why this car ride felt so different.

"Where are we going? Why isn't Daddy coming with us?" I blurted.

"Shhh! Be quiet. You'll wake your brother. Just lie down by your sister and go to sleep," my mother replied.

But I couldn't sleep. My confused mind raced with questions. Next week was to be my first day of school. I wondered what it would be like and whether or not our friends from across the street would be there. Or would we be far away?

I liked the boys across the street. They lived in a two-story, weathered-brown house with lots of room. Sometimes we played on the big, covered porch that ran along the front of their house. It gave cool shade when the sun was hot and kept us dry when it rained. A forest of old stumps and tall trees covered their backyard, where we imagined castles for kings and queens or pretended to be explorers on a safari. Each corner of their property filled our childhood dream world with adventure.

But now we were leaving.

Just as my eyes were giving way to the weight of sleep, the car slowed and turned into a driveway. Straight ahead of us, I could see a small, two-story, white building.

"You can make your call here at my house," I heard Aunt Irene say. "I'll wait in the car with the kids."

"You and Patsy stay put. I'll be right back," Mother ordered. She laid Bertie on the seat beside Aunt Irene and slipped out of the car. I watched her walk quickly through the rain and disappear into the house.

I don't remember much about that unfamiliar place. But I do remember the music on the car radio. It was a song I would come to hate, without fully knowing why:

I-rene, good-ni-i-ight.
I-rene, good night.
Good night, I-rene.
Good night, I-rene.
I'll see you in my dreams.

Soon the door of the house opened, and our mother returned. "It's all set," she said as she got back into the car.

"Mommy, I don't like it here. Why are we here?" I asked as my sister began to fuss. "Are we staying here? Are you staying with us?"

I was used to my mother going away and leaving me. But she always left me at Grandma's. And this wasn't Grandma's house.

"No, we can't stay here," she said, glancing toward Aunt Irene. "I just phoned Grandma. We're going to her house."

"Then why is Patsy crying?" I pushed. But nobody answered my six-year-old concern.

The big black car began moving again. It rumbled over the bumps in the road, and the light rain continued to bounce off the hood. It was Sunday, August 26, 1956. The next day would be my sister's fifth birthday.

After what seemed like forever, we turned down a street I recognized. "This is Grandma's road," I said eagerly as I strained my neck to see her house through the growing darkness.

The big black car slowed to a crawl and made a sharp right turn into the long, straight driveway.

"We're here. This is Grandma's house," I announced happily as the car came to a stop.

Grandma and Grandpa Imerson had built their humble home out of trees they had cleared from their land and cut into boards. When Grandpa died in May 1947, the house was incomplete. Now, almost ten years later, water was fetched from the outside well and the toilet facility was an outhouse at the end of a path leading away from the house. On the inside of the house, boards had not yet been applied to most of the uninsulated walls, and exposed studs revealed the outside wall boards. Bugs and mice tried to take up residence in the house, and cracks in the boards were stuffed with newspapers and rags to keep out the cold winter wind.

"Stay here, kids," my mother said as she got out and walked toward the back door of the house.

I reached over and rolled down the window to get a better look. The door of the house opened, and Grandma stepped out to the tiny, weathered porch that danced with light from the kitchen window.

Over her clothes she wore her usual full apron—the one with pretty pink flowers, dark pink edging, and a little pocket where she always kept a hanky. Without a word, she stepped down from the porch and walked straight to the car.

"Grandma," I sighed.

"Come along," she said as she opened the door to help us out. "Let's get you something to eat and then off to bed. You can stay with me tonight."

Mommy began to say something as she reached into the front seat to get our sleeping brother, but Grandma interrupted her. "Not now," she said. "We'll talk later."

Once our few belongings were piled into the corner of the kitchen and the big black car drove away, Grandma served us a snack of toast and homemade jelly. And then it was time for bed.

In the bedroom that was off of the kitchen, my sister and brother were tucked into the wood-frame double bed. Our mother would join them there later. I was sent to sleep in Grandma's room. Reflecting back as an adult, I'm not sure why I got to sleep with Grandma, except that the two of us always shared her bed when I stayed with her.

Lying quietly in her big brass bed, I strained to hear the hushed voices coming from the kitchen. I wanted to know why Mommy had bundled us all up and left so quickly, without letting us say "good-bye" to Daddy.

"I told you when you married him that you'd made your bed and would have to lie in it. Now, here you are on my doorstep with three small children."

"Mom, I can't live on that farm one more day. You don't know what I have to put up with. His father always spies on me. He even cut a hole in his hedge to watch me from their house across the field. No one can come or go without it being reported. It's like a prison. He didn't want us to get married, and now he's doing everything possible to drive us apart. Well—he has succeeded."

"You have to think about these children. What about them?" Grandma asked.

I tried to hear Mommy's answer but nothing filled the air until she broke the silence. "There's something else I need to tell you, and I know you're not going to like it."

There was another long pause.

"Mom, I'm going to have another baby."

As I drifted off to sleep, my mind was full of questions, but I was happy to be at Grandma's and tucked into her big brass bed. I was only six years old, but my short life's experiences already had taught me that as long as Grandma was around, everything would be OK.

In the years to come, I would find out just how important that secure knowledge was and the difference it would make in my life.

# CHAPTER 3

# Better to Have Loved

WHEN WE HURRIED away from our farmhouse on that August night in 1956, our family's world turned upside down. As children, our reality became life without a dad—something we were reminded of every day after we started school and discovered that we were the only kids at Harold Bishop Elementary without a dad.

I now realize that Grandma's world changed too. Her widow's home became a hive of activity. Every corner was overrun with the belongings and sounds of four more people. When I look at photos of that time, Grandma's face looks tired and shows the evidence of a life filled with sadness, loss, and concern.

Grandma was born Nancy Mabel Webb in Bishop's Stortford, Hertfordshire, England, on July 10, 1899. She was the first of eight children born to Ann and Edward Charles Webb, and she was known throughout her life as Mabel.

When she was two years old, the family moved to Rotherhithe, London, not far from where the *Mayflower* was built. At thirteen, she successfully completed her formal education and went into service as domestic help to Mr. and Mrs. Mills, who hired her as a kitchen hand for their small private London hotel that was known as *The Chandos*. She proved to be a trustworthy, hard worker and soon became head cook of their hotel.

Five years later, in 1919, the doctor ordered Mr. Mills to rest, and he and his wife moved to Hove, a seaside resort town along the south coast of England. Grandma went with them to serve as their cook and housekeeper.

In 1921, they returned to London, where Mr. and Mrs. Mills took over another private hotel known as *The Mayfair,* which was on Down Street. Tucked away in my files is a note from my great-aunt Hilda, who recalled Grandma's work at *The Mayfair* by saying, "I think Mabel just about ran the place. When she slept, I don't know."

During those years, Grandma worked eighteen-hour days, six-and-a-half days a week, and she had little time to socialize or spend time with family. Her half day off was spent visiting family one week and her best friend, Edie Green, the next week.

Life for Grandma revolved around work, until a friend gave Grandma's name and address to James Kinkaid, who was born in Aberdeen, Scotland, but lived and worked in Vancouver, Canada. Not long after they began corresponding, James, who was known by his friends as Kenny, proposed by mail and sent Mabel an engagement ring. To introduce her to what soon would become her home, he also sent photos of Vancouver and the west coast of Canada. Grandma accepted the proposal and committed to marry the man she knew only through letters and photos.

On April 7, 1928, she said "good-bye" to Mr. and Mrs. Mills, whom she had served for fifteen years. They tried to discourage her from leaving, but at twenty-eight years of age, her mind was made up. They did, however, stay connected with each other through mail until Mr. and Mrs. Mills died.

After a few days of packing and a going-away party with family and friends, Grandma said her final good-byes, walked with her dad along Platform 13 at London's Victoria Station, and boarded Car 13 of the train bound for Southhampton. It was Friday, April 13, 1928. She never would see her parents again.

At the end of the sixty-two-mile ride, she boarded the *SS Aurania* and began the ten-day trans-Atlantic voyage to Montreal, Canada, where she arrived on April 22.

Grandma was the first of her family to leave home for a foreign country where everything was different from what she was accustomed to and where she didn't know anyone. She did, however, know how to work hard and follow through with whatever she set her mind to. She had a determined and adventurous spirit that gave others the impression that she wasn't afraid of anything. But this courageous pioneer heart was soon to be put to the test.

Within six days of arriving in Montreal, Nancy Mabel Webb met her fiancé for the first time; traveled to Stratford, Ontario, for her wedding; and on April 28, 1928, became Mrs. James Kinkaid. On May 7, after spending the next few days in nearby Toronto, my grandparents-to-be boarded a train and traveled west across Canada to Vancouver, British Columbia, arriving at 7:30 A.M. on May 12, 1928.

Five and a half years after their marriage, Grandpa Kinkaid died on January 31, 1934, at the age of thirty-eight years. Not yet thirty-five, Grandma became a widow and faced the challenge of raising their four-year-old daughter, Doreen Mabel, who had been born on November 4, 1929. At a time when there was no government assistance for single moms or widows, and the whole world was struggling to survive the Great Depression, Grandma turned down her family's pleas for her to return to England so that they could help her raise her daughter.

Grandma later told me that because she had chosen to leave her family and come to Canada, she didn't believe it was right to go running back to them when things got tough. Instead, she worked hard to survive while her family sent care packages of clothing for "the child." Years later, I learned from my grandma's sisters that before they sent the parcels, they laundered the clothes and scuffed the shoes because they knew Grandma would not want them to sacrifice by sending brand-new things.

Grandma didn't talk about the hardships of those depression years as a single mom, and I also don't remember hearing her speak about the role that my grandfather's family did or did not have in her life during those years. She did, however, maintain some contact with a couple of them throughout her life. She also had a strong bond with her family, even though they were many miles away, and enjoyed a close friendship with Jack and Rose Macalister and their daughter, Flora, who all lived next door. Bit by bit, over the years, I gleaned snippets of information that told me she did whatever she could to put food on the table and keep a roof over her and her young daughter.

On December 3, 1941, almost eight years after my grandfather's death, Grandma married Hurlbert (Bert) Lloyd Imerson, who, by all accounts of those who knew him, was a hard-working, loving, and devoted husband and father. I don't know how they met, but when they married, Grandpa had been working in the northern community of Ft. St. James. He had two grown daughters who were living away from home and had families of their own.

Nine months after their marriage, Grandpa Imerson's six-year-old grandson, Herbie Hoover, came to live with them and became like a little brother to my mom, who was twelve at the time. Herbie's mom believed that he would receive a better education and be in a more solid home environment with Grandma and Grandpa than with her and the rest of the family in the tiny northern area of Willow River, British Columbia, where they lived.

Over the next four years, the blended family of four moved from Vancouver to Langley, British Columbia, and then to Westholme and Victoria on Vancouver Island. At each of the three locations, they lived on farms that Grandma and Grandpa managed for the owners.

Finally, on December 20, 1945, Grandma's detailed accounts show that they bought five acres of virgin land in Surrey, a community about twenty miles from Vancouver, British Columbia. They paid six hundred and seventy dollars for the property and moved there on February 19, 1946. Together they built a small structure they called home and began the manual task of clearing the land and living off what it produced—a far cry from the cultured, world-class city of London, England.

After only five-and-a-half years of marriage and fifteen months of working their own land, Grandpa Imerson suffered a fatal stroke. On May 12, 1947, exactly nineteen years to the day after Grandma's arrival in Vancouver, she was widowed for a second time and once again faced monumental choices and responsibilities. Grandma was forty-seven years old, my mom was sixteen years old, Herbie was eleven, and the home and land that Grandma and Grandpa had hoped to develop still needed a lot of work. The depth of Grandma's loss is evident in a short poem I found written in one of her notebooks:

No one knows my heartache
Only those who have lost can tell
Of the grief that I bear in silence
For the one I loved so well.

True to Grandma's indomitable spirit, and despite her grief and disappointment, she had the following poem written in Grandpa's obituary:

Every hour we dearly miss him,
Sadly do we feel his loss.
Lonely in our home without him,
Help us, Lord, to bear the Cross.
Christ will clasp the broken chain
Closer when we meet again.

Despite multiple uncertainties, Grandma remained strong and received help from her neighbors and friends at church. She also committed to keep Herbie with her, and send him home to his mom for summer visits.

Meanwhile, my mom, who had met a young man while working part-time at Spencer's Department Store before Grandpa died, continued to work.

A year and a half later, on January 29, 1949, Grandma's only child, my mom, married Trevor Patrick Davies Worrall. Fifteen months later, on May 2, 1950, Nancy Mabel Webb Kinkaid Imerson became a grandma for the first time.

Nancy Mabel Webb at
2 years old, 1901

Nancy Mabel Webb at 15 years old, 1914

James and Mabel Kinkaid on their
wedding day, April, 28, 1928

Mabel and her daughter, Doreen (7),
Summer 1937

Bert and Mabel Imerson, 1943

Doreen Kinkaid (16), August 1946

Mabel helping to build their home in
Surrey, BC, 1946

Mabel and Bert using a
buck saw and clearing their
land in Surrey, BC, 1946

Front view of the home
Mabel and Bert built in
Surrey, BC, May 1947

Back view of Mabel and Bert's home
in Surrey, BC. Herbie Hoover (11)
in foreground, 1947

Trevor Worrall (21) and Doreen
Kinkaid (17), May 1947

Herbie Hoover and
his step-grandma,
Mabel, circa 1948

# CHAPTER 4

# Light in the Darkness

I WAS BORN AT Langley Memorial Hospital and was barely two months old when my mom went back to work at Spencer's Department Store, which was across the river in New Westminster. Prior to getting married, she had been a cashier at the same store, but the successful Vancouver area chain recently had been acquired by the rival national giant, Eaton's Department Store. Mom's income was needed to supplement Dad's odd jobs and the work he did on his parents' farm, where he made fifteen dollars a month. While they both worked, someone needed to take care of the baby, so Grandma took me in.

From time to time, my parents picked me up from Grandma's and took me to their house on the farm. After a day or two, they returned me to Grandma. Her home became so familiar to me that only family photos prompt small memories of the days my parents took me to be with them. Grandma's home was my home.

During my baby and toddler years with Grandma, I was introduced to Herbie, who still lived with Grandma at the time. As a boy, he was a prankster and often got into trouble for his mischievous antics, but he was loved by all who knew him. I don't remember being teased by him, but he recalls that Grandma used to get upset with him when he teased me through a hole in the wall that divided his tiny room from Grandma's bedroom, where I was supposed to be going to sleep.

In September of 1950, when Herbie was only fourteen years old, Grandma got word that his thirty-five-year-old mother had been killed in a car accident. Herbie did not attend his mom's funeral and remained with Grandma for the next two years. Then in her diary entry of June 23, 1952, she simply wrote, "Sent Herbie home." He had been with her for ten years and experienced the loss of his grandpa and his mom while in Grandma's care.

As Herbie grew older and had a family of his own, he and Grandma continued to have a loving connection with each other. Every time he dropped by for a visit, I'd see her face light up with a broad smile as he threw his arms around her and said, "Hi, Grandma. Did you miss me?" Then, with a twinkle in his eye, he teasingly told her how young she still looked. Even in his senior years, Herbie spoke fondly of Grandma and the difference she had made in his life.

By the evening of August 26, 1956, when my mom arrived at Grandma's with the three of us children in the big black car, I had lived most of my life with Grandma. And though I'm not sure of all the reasons why Grandma took me in so often and from as young as two months old, it appears that Mom's work and second pregnancy, followed by the birth of my sister, contributed to it. Regardless of the reasons, it was during those early years that a close bond began to form between Grandma and me—a bond that became my anchor for years to come.

During my toddler and preschool years, we became a permanent part of each others' everyday lives. Wherever Grandma went, I went—except on Tuesdays. Every Tuesday, she got up earlier than usual, and by the time she came to wake me at 5:30 in the morning, she already had been up for an hour preparing for the long day ahead.

"Come on, Ann, time to get up."

"Where we going, Grandma?" I asked in my sleepy toddler voice.

"I'm going to help Uncle Jack and Auntie Flora at their house."

"Why?"

"Because I said I would help them."

"Why?"

"Come along now. There's a good girl." she urged. "I can't miss the bus. I know it's early, but when we get to Mr. and Mrs. Reimer's house, you can have a bit of breakfast and go back to sleep."

Uncle Jack and Aunt Flora weren't really my aunt and uncle. They had been helpful neighbors of Grandma's during her years as a widow with a young child. Uncle Jack's wife, Rose, had been Grandma's close friend until she passed away almost two years after Grandpa Imerson died. Flora, who was now grown and working, was their only child and never married or had children of her own. She was nine years older than my mom and shared a house with her dad.

Once a week, Grandma made the long trek to Uncle Jack and Aunt Flora's to clean their house. While her work met a need for them, I sometimes think they had Grandma come because they wanted to help her financially and knew she'd accept their help more if she did something for it.

On Tuesdays during the winter, Grandma and I were on the road before sunrise. She didn't like to rush around early in the morning, so everything was organized the night before. In one bag, she put some things for herself: a floral, bib-style apron, a change of shoes, an umbrella in case it rained, and her little silver flashlight. In the second bag, she put everything I needed, which included a change of clothes, books, and my brown and white teddy bear that had button eyes and a stitched mouth.

When we were ready to leave, Grandma hung the two bags on her left arm, and we stepped outside into the cool air. Once she locked the door, she reached down and lifted me up. She then carried me most of the two blocks down the quiet country road that was waiting for the morning sun. At the end of what was known as Clow Road, we turned right and walked another half block along Hjorth Road to the Reimers' house.

When she knew I was settled, Grandma walked a half mile or so to catch the only bus that passed that way in the morning. From there she traveled over country roads, across the Patullo Bridge that spanned the Fraser River, and through the streets of New Westminster, Burnaby, and Vancouver. After she changed buses in Vancouver, her journey continued on over the Lions Gate Bridge and through city streets until she arrived at her stop in prestigious West Vancouver. From there, she walked four blocks up a long, steep, partially paved road, turned right, and walked a block east on Inglewood Avenue to Uncle Jack and Aunt Flora's beautiful home surrounded by manicured lawns and flower gardens. The whole trip took about three hours.

After resting for a few minutes with a cup of hot tea, she spent the next six hours working on the list of chores Aunt Flora had left earlier that morning. By the end of the day, I'm sure she felt tired as she exchanged house shoes for walking shoes, put on her coat and gloves, tied a kerchief around her head to stay warm, and walked back down the hill. Boarding the late afternoon bus, she retraced the same three-hour trip she had made earlier that day.

Throughout most of the year it was dark when she left home in the morning, and it was dark when she stepped off the bus at the end of her return trip where Johnston and Hjorth Roads met. Today it's a busy shopping area known as Guildford. For the final leg of her journey, I can imagine her stepping off the bus, pulling the little silver flashlight from her bag, and walking the remaining half mile along the dirt road that passed through a heavily wooded area to the Reimers' house, where she had left me twelve hours earlier.

I was told that, although I was very young, I knew exactly when it was time for Grandma to come home. I'd stand on the couch at the big front window, and when I saw a light bouncing through the darkness, I'd proclaim, "Grandma! Grandma's home."

# CHAPTER 5

# Mystery Man at the Well

ON APRIL 3, 1957, Mom gave birth to my brother Ian, bringing the number of children in our family to four and making Grandma's tiny four-room home seem even smaller. It was just over seven months since we had invaded her peaceful world.

Prior to Ian's arrival, a man moved into the building at the back of Grandma's property. Over the years, it had been home to chickens, tools, and equipment. But since Grandpa Imerson's death, it had become shrouded with vines and bushes and overrun by bugs and rodents that made their home in the few belongings still stored there.

Among those treasures were a solid oak table that matched the chairs in Grandma's kitchen but did not fit into her tiny house and a gramophone that I don't remember ever hearing play the old records stacked in a box beside it. There also were a number of books packed in crates, with mold forming on their neglected pages, a copper tub washing machine powered by a gasoline engine, and other items stored for safekeeping.

Once the shed was roughly converted into what one would be hard-pressed to call a home, the man took up residence and, for a number of months, occupied our mother's time and affection—until one day, he disappeared.

Years later, when I was an adult, my mother told me that the police had stopped the man and her when they were coming home from a party one night. He was arrested and sentenced to ten years in prison for something to do with drugs and other things she didn't want to talk about.

I sometimes wonder why Grandma allowed the man to stay on her property. Then I wonder if she was helpless to do anything about it. I'll never know, although it's hard for me to think of my grandma as helpless.

There isn't much that I remember about the man, except for his name and one event that is vividly stamped into my memory. Sometimes it seems more like a bad nightmare.

One morning, I heard shouting and screaming coming from outside the back of Grandma's house. When I looked out, I saw the man from the shed standing by the well, which was just outside the kitchen window. His arms were stretched out over the open well, with my little brother Bert dangling from his clenched hands. Only three years old, Bert cried out as he hung upside down over the water below, and the man threatened to drop him into the well if he ever wet the bed again.

I don't recall how I reacted at the time, but when I had children of my own and they wet their beds, the image of the man, my brother, and the well rushed back to my mind. I told myself that it didn't matter that they wet their beds. They too would grow out of it.

Saturday nights were usually bath nights at Grandma's house. The round galvanized tub was taken down from the nail on the outside of the house and placed in the middle of the kitchen floor by the stove for us to bathe in. Because the water in the tub cooled while we were sitting in it, hot water was added from the simmering kettle on the stove as needed. The youngest child always had his bath first, followed by each one up the line. By the time it was my turn, the water could be light brown or dark brown, depending on how dirty my younger brothers and sister had become throughout the week.

Later, when Grandma got indoor plumbing, some of our everyday living changed, including the Saturday night bath ritual. But while the *how* of bathing was altered, the night we bathed never did. According to Grandma, Saturday night was shine-your-shoes and take-a-bath night. And that's exactly what we did—whether we thought we needed it or not!

The new plumbing also meant that it was no longer necessary to draw water from the outside well. Before it was boarded up and nailed shut permanently, it was filled with old cans and bottles and some roots and rocks from the garden. It took a long time to fill the deep well, but eventually, it was sealed tightly.

The man was gone. The well was sealed. It never would be used again—by anyone or for anything.

# CHAPTER 6

# Where There's a Will, There's a Way

FOR GRANDMA, MISSING church was unthinkable. And because I had spent most of my life with her, she had instilled the same habit in me. Sundays were always the day that people put on their Sunday best, no matter what their best might be, and they went to church.

When Sundays arrived, I eagerly put on my dress that was reserved for special days and walked with Grandma to Hjorth Road Mission Church, where we attended Sunday school and morning services. I don't remember my mom ever coming with us, but sometimes my sister and brothers did.

One Sunday, when I was seven years old, it was announced that any child who memorized ten Bible verses and recited them in front of the whole congregation would win his or her very own Bible. Even when I was a child, I liked contests and challenges. So with Grandma's help and encouragement, I worked hard to perfect each verse. In my memory, I still can see myself pacing back and forth in the backyard, repeating each reference and verse over and over again until I got it right.

When I was ready, the date was arranged for me to recite the ten verses in front of the people. Like all other Sundays, I put on my Sunday dress and walked with Grandma to the little brown church. We made our way along Clow Road to Eddie and Ivy Anhorn's home, where we cut through the yard to a path that connected their property with the senior Anhorns' property, which was next to the church.

Paul and Eva Anhorn, the senior Anhorns, had started a Sunday school in their home for their children and those who lived nearby. Over time, they also started holding church services in their living room. When the room could no longer hold the number of people attending, Mr. and Mrs. Anhorn donated the property next to their home and built a church out of wood that Mr. Anhorn, who was a commercial fisherman, salvaged from the Fraser River.

I'm told that I, as a young girl, often stood at the bottom of the steep wood stairs leading to the front door of the church and waited for older people to arrive. When they started up the stairs, I offered my arm, and they graciously allowed me to help, as if my tiny frame was strong enough to support them. But on this morning, I didn't stop at the bottom of the stairs when Grandma and I arrived at the church.

After the opening formalities and singing, my name was announced. I walked up the bare wood floor aisle toward the front of the church and stepped onto the raised platform. As I stood alone on the only piece of carpet in the whole building, I began to recount each verse in the order I had memorized them from the *King James Version* of the Bible. Some of those verses were:

For God so loved the world, that He gave His only begotten Son, that whosoever believeth in Him should not perish, but have everlasting life.

—John 3:16

Jesus saith unto him, I am the way, the truth, and the life; no man cometh unto the Father, but by me.

—John 14:6

If we confess our sins, he is faithful and just to forgive us our sins, and to cleanse us from all unrighteousness.

—1 John 1:9

When I stumbled on the words and panic flashed through me, I looked past the people lining the simple wood benches and focused on my grandma, who was, as always, sitting on the left by the center aisle, three rows up from the back of the small church.

Grandma didn't offer many verbal expressions of approval, but when she smiled and nodded slightly from that back pew, I felt sure that I could do exactly what I was up there to do. When I finished the last verse, a smile that shone through her eyes told me that she was proud of my accomplishment. I had won my Bible.

While my mom, sister, brothers, and I lived with Grandma, our dad continued living in the house we had left that rainy August night. His long-haul trucking job took him out of town a lot, but I'm told that he sometimes dropped in at Grandma's to see us. I have no memory of those visits, but I've learned that whenever they took place, Mom went out and Grandma stayed with us.

Throughout those years, Grandma always was busy with a life that must have felt chaotic at times and a home that was overrun with children and activity. But she never made me feel like I was in the way or an inconvenience. She also didn't use her busy household as an excuse to back out of the scheduled meetings I found marked in her annual calendars that served as diaries. In some ways, I wonder if those commitments away from home provided a bit of respite for her.

The meetings listed on Grandma's calendars included a number of church board and congregational meetings that were held to discuss a merger between Hjorth Road Mission Church, of which she was a member, and Green Timbers Mission Church. At the time, Grandma served on the Hjorth Road Mission Church board and, as such, was involved in formulating the details of the merger. I have no doubt that her organizational skills, attention to detail, and calm spirit were appreciated and played an important role during the merger talks.

On Friday, April 4, 1958, the official sod-turning took place on a piece of property located halfway between the two churches. Six months later, on October 19, the first service of Johnston Heights Evangelical Free Church was held in the new church building. It was a new beginning for a small group of people who were destined to multiply and continue serving God in a growing community. Since that first Sunday service, Johnston Heights has been home to many, many people and continues to thrive as a vibrant, God-honoring church that is actively serving the community.

When Grandma saw a job that needed to be done, she rallied to it. It didn't matter how lofty or menial the task seemed. It simply was something that needed to be taken care of. In fact, after she fulfilled her role as a board member during the merger of her small mission church with the other similar congregation, she took on the janitorial responsibilities for the newly formed church.

For a couple of years, every other Saturday or so, she walked three miles on gravel roads to the new church. She dusted, washed, swept, and cleaned the upper and lower floors of the church from top to bottom. Then she walked the three miles back home.

Occasionally, I went with her, although, in retrospect, I'm not sure how helpful I was as a young girl. On our walk to the church, she told me about how her neighborhood had changed over the years—from a two-rut mud or dirt trail, depending on the season, to a gravel road that was now sprayed with black oil every summer to keep the dust down. She also pointed out that there were fewer trees now because more people were building houses and moving into the area.

When we arrived at the church, we dusted the pews, picked up loose papers that had been left behind, straightened hymn books in the holders on the back of each pew, and pushed a mop up and down each aisle and under each pew to clean the linoleum floors of the sanctuary. When the upstairs was cleaned thoroughly, we moved downstairs. In the main open area, we placed chairs and small benches on the tops of tables so that we could sweep the cement floors after Grandma sprinkled a green cleaning sand on them to keep the dust at a minimum. We also cleaned the kitchen and each of the rooms that surrounded the open area before scrubbing the bathroom floors, sinks, and toilets.

We were usually too tired to talk much as we made our way home. If I said anything about being tired, she told me how important it was to complete whatever job we committed to, no matter how tired we felt. Then she added, "Where there's a will, there's a way."

Grandma was hard working, took her responsibilities seriously, and struggled to understand why people would say they'd do something and then not follow through. When it came to getting a job done, people could always depend on her. And she liked it that way. By her actions, she showed me what it meant to be faithful to my commitments—regardless of difficulties or circumstances.

But on Saturday, October 24, 1959, circumstances won out. That morning, I woke up not feeling well and could not go with Grandma to help clean the church as we had planned. When she returned later in the afternoon, I was lying on the couch and unable to use the right side of my body. My arm and leg felt like they had heavy weights attached to them.

Grandma's diaries indicate that I was admitted to the hospital on the 24th, discharged on the 26th, and readmitted on the 30th. The doctors were concerned that I had polio, but after numerous tests, they said that I was in the clear. I have no recollection of my time in the hospital except for being poked and prodded. My sister, however, recalls walking into my room, seeing me stretched out on the bed in full traction with weights attached to each of my limbs, and being told that she could not come close to me. When I was released from the hospital on November 4, I still was unable to use the right side of my body, and the doctors had no explanation for my continuing paralysis.

The day after my hospital release, our neighbor, Ivy Anhorn, suggested I go to a chiropractor. Chiropractic treatments were almost unheard of in the late fifties, and I believe Dr. Mehl was the only chiropractor in the area at that time. In desperation, I was carried into his office, had x-rays and treatments, spent most of the day there, and later walked out on my own strength. After two and a half weeks of hospitals and doctors, I finally was able to walk.

I can't help but think that many prayers and Grandma's words, "Where there's a will, there's a way," rang loud and clear during those uncertain weeks.

# CHAPTER 7

# Grandma's Brass Bed

A S A YOUNG girl, I was curious about the old secretariat and the few delicate possessions Grandma kept behind its tall beveled glass door. The heavy piece of furniture looked like it was made of authentic tiger oak, which I later learned was produced by quarter cutting golden oak to produce the prominent "tiger eye" design. In reality, Grandma's secretariat was built with some other kind of wood that had been made to look exotic by using a faux tiger oak staining process that was made popular in the early nineteen hundreds. It was the poor man's version of the real thing.

Today, the stately secretariat stands tall in my home and reminds me of the many conversations Grandma and I shared while we looked at the keepsakes she had tucked away inside.

When we were young, Grandma rarely removed the cups and saucers or special ornaments from the cabinet. And she only allowed my sister and me to look at them through the glass door. As we grew older, she let us open the cabinet and look at, but not touch, her treasures. When we asked questions about them, her eyes came alive as she recounted the special memories that lived within each piece.

In my latter teen years, she removed specific items from the cabinet and, after retelling the stories, turned each piece upside down and showed me the handwritten tag that indicated who it was to go to when she died. My name was on some of those pieces, but at the time, only one of her possessions held special meaning for me. And it was too big to go in the cabinet.

"Grandma, you're going to live to be at least ninety years old," I'd announce whenever she reminded me which piece went to which friend or family member. "The only thing I really hope you'll leave me is your brass bed."

She never told me that it would be mine, but somehow I knew it would.

When Grandma and Grandpa Kinkaid were married in Ontario, Canada, in 1928, they bought the second-hand solid brass bed and brought it with them when they moved to the west coast right after their wedding.

While I was growing up, it became the bed that I shared with Grandma, and it also doubled as my secret hiding place for bits of money that I earned. I would wrap my earnings in a plastic bag, remove the round top from one of the bedposts, and stash the money in the opening. To ensure that my treasure wouldn't fall to the bottom of the long, brass post, I taped a piece of cardboard across the opening, about six inches down, before placing my money inside. Only Grandma and I knew about my secret hiding place.

What really mattered most to me were the memories I had of being in that bed. From the time I was very young, I shared Grandma's brass bed with her. Cold winter nights in her home that had no central heating always were cozier when she placed the hot water bottle between the covers to warm the bed before we got in. Once we were snuggled in, the weight and warmth of the flannel sheets, wool blankets, and goose down comforter kept us toasty warm. It was a feeling that made it hard to crawl out of bed in the morning to get dressed in the cold air that waited for the heat of the morning fire.

For me, Grandma's bed was a safe and comforting place.

I loved to lie beside her in the darkness and listen as she told stories of growing up and working in England. There wasn't a lot of laughter in the stories, and she especially seemed to avoid saying much about the first few years following her arrival in Canada.

It also became a classroom of sorts, a place where I discovered answers to the never-ending questions that came from my curious mind. I learned how to ask the right questions and never gave up wanting to know as much as I could about this person whom I loved very much and whose life had become so intertwined with mine.

I'd ask questions like: "Grandma, what was it like in England during the First World War?" "How did you come to live in Canada?" "Grandpa died before I was born—what was he like?" "Why was my mom an only child?"

What I learned was not always found in those hushed conversations, however. Every night, I watched Grandma get into bed and reach for her well-worn Bible. In it was the small *Daily Bread* devotional book, from which she read one page and the corresponding passage of Scripture, followed by a chapter or so from her Bible. In her lifetime, she read it from cover to cover many times.

When she finished reading, she laid her Bible in its place and reached for the glycerin with rose water hand lotion that always sat on her bedside table. She squeezed a little out from the tube, set the container down, and spread the lotion up her arms, being careful to rub some of the sweet-smelling aroma on her elbows. After she massaged her hands—the softest hands I ever held—she removed her glasses, placed them on top of her Bible, and turned off the lamp that hung over our heads on the bed frame.

Before she rolled onto her right side to sleep, we often talked quietly in the darkness about school or what it was like to live in England or the family she left behind. I could tell by the sound of her voice that she missed them, but then she'd add, "Never mind. Everything in its time."

Looking back, I believe that Grandma's actions and habits helped to give me stability in the middle of my roller-coaster life of change and emotion. I didn't understand it at the time, but now as an adult, I often reflect on what she showed me through her everyday life—even in her bedtime routine. Her commitment and the example she lived helped to make me feel secure. I didn't see her dwell on the negative circumstances or sad events of her life. She simply dealt with them and moved on. And while she wasn't one to talk a lot about her personal relationship with God, she certainly lived it.

Later, Grandma's brass bed became mine and found its place in our home. It served as our teenage daughter's bed, was used by her and her husband when they got married, and later became their daughter's bed. Next, it went into storage for a time, before we again found room for it to stand proudly in our guest room.

It may seem odd that I struggled with the idea of ever parting with Grandma's brass bed. It held countless memories and had followed five generations of my family. Whenever I looked at it or lay on it, I was reminded of the conversations Grandma and I shared at the end of long days and what I learned in the warmth and safety of her brass bed.

Any time our grandchildren stayed overnight with us they slept in my grandma's brass bed. Our son's daughter, Calista, especially liked me to sit or lie on the bed with her and answer the many questions she had about the generations of family whose photos hung on the wall at the foot of the bed. I'd recount the stories I'd heard while growing up and how she fit within the family mosaic.

By the time we moved into a smaller home, Calista was twelve years old and had fallen in love with Grandma's brass bed. It was then that it officially moved to the fifth generation and found a new home in our granddaughter's room. When I stood in Calista's room and looked at how it had been dressed up to suit a teenager's room, I couldn't help but recall those private moments Grandma and I had shared together and that I had shared with my grandchildren.

# CHAPTER 8

# The Good and Bad of Change

FTER MY PARENTS had been separated for almost three years, Grandma convinced them to get back together "for the sake of the children." By this time, Mom and Dad were speaking to one another, and Mom was pregnant again.

Sometime in the spring of 1959, a few months before my polio scare, Dad moved in with us. That was followed by my ninth birthday and the birth of another boy on May 28. Baby Keith brought the total number of people crowded together in Grandma's tiny, unfinished, two-bedroom bungalow to three adults and five children. I don't know how the sleeping arrangements were decided, but my parents, sister, and three brothers all shared one bedroom, and I slept with Grandma in her room.

When Dad moved into Grandma's house with us, a lot of things changed, including Sunday mornings.

Even when he was a boy, Dad had never attended church. Mom, on the other hand, had. And as a young teenager, she had been confirmed in the Anglican Church. Throughout her childhood and teen years, she was involved in church youth activities. A short chronology listed in the back of Grandma's Bible gives testimony to how important Mom's spiritual life was to Grandma and possibly how important it once had been to my mom. The notations read:

Doreen Mabel Ann Rose Kinkaid
Born—November 4, 1929
Baptized—April 22, 1934
Confirmed—April 29, 1945
Accepted Christ—June 5, 1946
Call to service—June 30, 1946

Three other dates are not noted here, but I can't help but wonder how they affected my mom's life choices. Those dates are the death of her father, when she was four years old; Grandma's second marriage, which gave Mom, at the age of twelve, a stepfather she adored; and her stepfather's sudden passing in May of 1947, when she was seventeen.

Sometime before Mom and Dad were married in January of 1949, Mom stopped going to church, and throughout most of my life, she was outwardly opposed to anything that involved church. It would be decades before she would return to her childhood church roots.

But despite the passage of time and the tumultuous relationship my mom and grandma had in their adult years, Grandma always carried a beautiful photo of my mom in her Bible. The photo had been taken outside on a sunny spring day, when my mom was sixteen years old. She wore a beautiful, yet simple, white dress and held her Bible close to her. Whenever I saw the photo, Grandma said, "That's when she was a good girl." It was her favorite photo of my mom.

Whether it was in spite of or because of this history, Mom didn't seem to mind that Grandma took me and my brothers and sister—when they wanted to go—to church and Sunday school while we were living in her home. But when Dad moved in with us, my parents agreed that they no longer wanted Grandma to take us to church. My brothers didn't seem to mind, possibly because they were so young, and my sister usually did what Mom told her. I, on the other hand, wanted to go with Grandma, and she made it clear that she wanted me to go with her. At church and Sunday school, I loved learning the Bible verses, doing the weekly lessons, singing the songs, and being with the people.

It didn't take long for Sunday mornings to become explosive tug-of-war events, pitting will against will.

"Ann, go change into your play clothes. You're not going to church with your grandmother," my mother said when she came out of the back bedroom and into the kitchen, dressed in her housecoat.

"Why not? I want to go."

"You're not going. That's all there is to it. Now, go do as you're told."

"But I want to go. Grandma says I can go. I got my Sunday school lesson done and everything."

"I don't care. Just go change your clothes, and don't wake your father."

From the front bedroom that Grandma and I shared off the living room, Grandma came and stood in the doorway leading to the kitchen. She usually wore a pretty floral dress with a matching short jacket or sweater. This morning was no exception. She was ready for church.

"What's the matter?" she asked.

"Ann's not going with you today," my mother replied. "There are better things for her to do here at home."

"What do you mean she's not going? Of course, she's going," insisted Grandma. "It's Sunday. It's time for church."

But my mother argued, "Her father and I discussed it and decided that she's staying home with the rest of the kids. We're her parents. We say what she can and can't do. And that's all there is to it."

Grandma didn't like confrontation, but I could see her back straighten and her shoulders draw back. "No, that's not all there is to it. She's singing in the children's choir today. And it wouldn't hurt you to come to church once in a while either. You used to, you know."

"I don't care what you want," my mother shot back. "It's what *we* want. We're her parents. She can stay home and do something around here today."

Grandma took an unyielding step forward and put her hand around my shoulder, "Come on, Ann. We have to go, or we'll be late."

"She's not going," yelled my mother as she stepped toward us and grabbed my arm. "You're staying home, young lady. You're getting too high and mighty for your own good. You're not going anywhere."

With all the commotion, my father appeared from behind the curtain leading to the back bedroom on the other side of the kitchen. Dressed in his trademark trucker overalls, his tall, muscular frame filled the doorway. His bottom lip protruded slightly as it pressed tightly against his top lip, accenting his firm jaw. Pointing sharply in the direction of my mother, he turned toward me and scowled. "Ann, you listen to your mother." Then, turning his steely blue eyes toward Grandma, he growled, "And you stay out of this, woman."

"She's our daughter," continued my mother. "She'll do as we tell her, and that's final."

Like a badger protecting its young, Grandma didn't look like she was about to give in. I watched her neck stiffen and her cheeks flare red. "No, it's not final," she said firmly. "All of you are living in my house and eating my food. If Ann wants to come to church with me, then she's going to come. And *that's* final."

I don't remember ever missing church during those years.

Later, buried in one of Grandma's books, I found a note that I wrote and gave to Grandma when I was nine years old. It read, "When you die, I hope you will go to heaven, and I hope you know I love you." It's clear that the bond between us was strong and growing stronger.

I never heard Grandma complain to anyone about her situation, especially to her family in England. But one day in early 1961, she received a letter that said her brother and his wife were coming for a visit in July. It would be the first reunion with any of her family since she left England more than thirty years before.

The visit meant that major changes had to take place—changes like finishing walls and painting inside and outside the house, digging a septic tank area, and building an addition for a pantry with a sink and running water and an indoor bathroom so the outhouse could be retired. With our sizable family living in Grandma's tiny home, there was a lot that had been left undone. The house now needed some tender loving care before the arrival of my great uncle and aunt. Our family had to move—soon.

On my brother Keith's second birthday, May 28, 1961, my parents and brothers moved into a new unfinished house three blocks from Grandma's home. Grandma now had six weeks to complete building projects, paint walls, organize rooms, redo curtains, and repair the many things that needed to be fixed. My sister, who had just had her appendix removed, stayed with Grandma for an extra week. I stayed for another month.

Then, almost five years after our family had landed on Grandma's doorstep and just past my eleventh birthday, I left the security of Grandma's home that had become my home. That night, I made a choice that would affect the rest of my life.

## PERSONAL REFLECTION

1.  What do you remember about your grandparents' home? If you were never in their home, what do you imagine it was like?

2.  What would you like your grandchildren to remember about your home? How will you create those memories?

3.  What do you know about your grandma and/or grandpa's life journey? What is most significant to you about their life journey?

4.  What qualities or habits did you see demonstrated in your grandmother or grandfather? Which ones are evident in your life? Which ones would you like to see in your grandchildren?

5.  Write a short letter to one or all of your grandchildren. If you don't have grandchildren, what do you imagine writing to them? Why not write it now in advance of their birth so they can read it later?

# CHAPTER 9

# Secret Vow of a Child

I T WAS LATE afternoon when I gave Grandma a hug and kiss at the door and started walking down the long dirt driveway toward the road that would take me away from the safety of Grandma's arms and the warmth of her home. After today, I no longer would be able to run to her or hear, "Chin up. Everything will be all right."

*This must be what it feels like to bleed on the inside*, I thought, *because it sure hurts in there right now.*

At the end of the driveway, I stopped at the silver-painted mailbox that stood guard from the top of its weathered wood post. As I reached to check inside the box, the letters "H. L. Imerson" stood out bold and black on the side of the box. Grandpa had been dead for fourteen years, but his initials remained in front of my grandparents' last name.

I had learned that when the mailbox was turned out and pointing across the road, it meant that Grandma had put a letter inside for the mailman to take to the post office or he had left mail for her. That afternoon, I didn't pay attention to where the box was facing. I lifted the hinged metal door on the end of the box and peered inside. Nothing.

Looking back up the driveway toward the house, I saw Grandma standing tall in her familiar bibbed apron that protected a simple, below-the-knee house dress. Even though green was her favorite color, her aprons were usually pink or blue floral, with edging to match, and coordinated with the dress she wore. Heavy elastic support stockings under full-length sheer nylons interrupted the flow of color and blended into the dark heeled slippers she wore around the house.

Before she came to Canada, Grandma had worked at jobs where she was on her feet eighteen hours a day, six and a half days a week. To protect her legs, she had worn heavy elastic stockings—a part of her wardrobe that never changed over the years, even during the hot summer months.

"Bye, Grandma," I yelled as I closed the door of the mailbox.

"Bye, Honey. Be a good girl."

"I love you, Grandma," I replied softly, choking back the lump that had formed in my throat.

Four years and nine months before, on a dark, rainy night, my mother had left my father and taken me and my younger sister and brother to live with Grandma in her tiny, four-room bungalow. I was only six years old and set to start school in one week. Over those years, the walls of Grandma's house strained against our growing family. Three children became five children, and one parent became two parents when Dad joined us. But there was always only one Grandma.

Before my family left for their new house, my mother reminded me that my place was with my parents. But I wasn't convinced.

"Why do I have to leave Grandma?" I muttered to myself. "Even with Great Uncle Harry and Great Aunt Lillian coming from England, Grandma and I could share her brass bed. I wouldn't be any trouble."

But adult minds were made up. The extra month that I was allowed to stay with Grandma after my family moved to their own house had gone by quickly. And as the time for me to leave her drew closer, I wished that time would stop.

The day before I had to leave, I overheard Grandma on the phone with my mom. I couldn't hear what was being said on the other end of the conversation, but Grandma's voice sounded sad.

"All right, one more day, and I'll send her to you," Grandma had said. But when the day arrived, I waited until the last moment to leave.

Turning from the mailbox, I walked along the gravel road that bordered the front of Grandma's property. I couldn't stop waving goodbye. Each time I looked back toward her house, Grandma was still there with her arm raised to the sky. A few more steps and she would be completely out of sight behind the neighbor's house, which stood closer to the road than Grandma's. I stopped, turned, and gave one last wave. Grandma's arm swayed back and forth in the air and then dropped to her side. Turning back to the road, I kicked at a small rock, sending it sideways into the weeds.

The house my parents bought needed a lot of work. The original owner had built the stucco and wood, three-bedroom rancher on a corner city lot and had finished only the outside. Inside the house, two-by-four studs outlined the rooms of the shell that never had been lived in.

Before moving in, my father had constructed walls by nailing sheet rock to the studs, but he had not yet taped and plastered the exposed nails and cracks where the sheets met. The floors were bare, unpainted plywood, as were the open cupboards and shelves throughout the house. The only doors were those leading outside from the front and back of the house. Even the bathroom had no door, except for a gray blanket that suggested privacy.

One bedroom was used for storage, another for our parents, and the third for the five of us kids. My brothers, sister, and I shared the one bedroom referred to as "the kids' room," where one old mattress lay on the floor.

Over the next three years, two more boys would be born into our family, making seven children in the house. But the interior construction remained much the same as when we first moved in.

Eventually, my parents got bunk beds for the boys and cleared the third bedroom for my sister and me to share. But when we moved into the house, we were told, "Be satisfied with what you have."

My first night in that house is etched permanently in my memory. The old, well-used mattress that lay on the floor of our bedroom had been discarded by its previous owner. It reeked of the pungent odor of dried urine and was where my sister and three brothers and I slept. In time, the stench mingled with second-hand cigarette smoke and washed the unpainted walls a yellowish gray.

In the hallway that ran down the center of the house, a single light bulb hung from the ceiling and cast a dim light into the bedroom. Eerie shadows crept up the walls to taunt the gray-wool blanket that covered the window. Dusty, unopened boxes spilled out from the bedroom closet, while the contents of boxes that had been unpacked lay in a jumble on the floor. The only sound I heard was my parents' voices coming from the kitchen at the other end of the hall. They were arguing—again.

I closed my eyes and thought about how different this felt from when I was in Grandma's home. I tried to imagine snuggling under the warm down-filled comforter on her bed and listening to the muted sounds of songs like "How Much Is That Doggie in the Window?" playing from her radio on the kitchen table.

*Soon Grandma will come to bed, and I will smell the sweet fragrance of her hand lotion*, I imagined. But as I rolled over on the mattress, reality captured my senses. I pressed toward the wall, buried my face in my arm, and cried.

"Mommy," my sister called out.

"What is going on?" my mother demanded as she made her way down the hall to our room. "You kids are supposed to be going to sleep."

As I turned to face the doorway, Mom stood there like a giant, with the hallway light behind her casting a glow around her shape. She took a couple of steps into the room and looked down at me. "What's the matter with you?" she asked roughly. "What are you crying about?"

"I miss Grandma," I replied as I rubbed the back of my hand over my tear-filled eyes. "Why can't I stay with Grandma?"

"Don't be ridiculous," she snapped. "This is your home now. Forget about Grandma, and go to sleep."

"But I miss her."

"I don't care. This is where you belong. Now go to sleep." With that, she turned and walked out of the room.

I lay on the mattress feeling betrayed and alone and wishing I had a say in where I lived. But nobody seemed to care what I thought or what I wanted. No one noticed a little girl who felt abandoned and empty in a people-filled house.

That night, having just turned eleven years old, I made a vow that is one of the clearest memories of my childhood. I brushed the remaining tears from my face, and without thinking of the consequences, I whispered into the darkness, "No one will ever again see how I feel on the inside. I will never cry again. Never."

# CHAPTER 10

# The Unspoken Cost

I N NOVEMBER OF 1961, just five months after we moved into the new house, Mom was diagnosed with hepatitis, apparently due to unsanitary conditions. All of us children, along with Dad, were immunized immediately, but it was too late for Dad. Within a couple of days, he too was told he had contracted the infectious disease.

Since both of our parents were restricted to bed, leaving five children between the ages of two and eleven to fend for themselves, Grandma came to our rescue—again. Early each morning, she walked three blocks to our house to do the laundry, cooking, and cleaning. Then she took care of Ian, Keith, and our parents while Bert, Pat, and I went to school. When the evening meal was finished and the youngest ones were ready for bed, she walked back home—with her little silver flashlight to guide her way.

It was up to each of us to do our homework in the evenings and to get ourselves ready for school in the mornings. My sister and I also looked after all the house and family needs during the weekends and on Tuesdays, when Grandma went to Flora's or worked as District Returning Officer for the government election.

She took this job very seriously, as it was her responsibility to ensure that proper procedures were followed at the station she was assigned to for any given election—municipal, provincial, or national. Years later, on September 16, 1980, after she gave notice that she no longer could continue working on the elections, she received a letter of commendation for an unprecedented thirty-three years of continuous service.

One positive highlight from my parents' time of illness was when Mom taught Pat and me how to play cribbage. When our parents began to feel better but still were restricted to bed, they played cards together. When they got tired of competing with each other, Mom decided to teach us. Being a natural competitor, I loved learning this game.

Two and a half weeks into my parents' illness, Grandma fell down our outside back stairs and injured her leg. I don't know if anyone realized how badly she was hurt because she kept on working just as hard as she had before her fall, walking to and from her home to our house, keeping up with church and community commitments and traveling to Uncle Jack and Aunt Flora's for her weekly day of work.

On Monday, December 11, a full ten days after Grandma's fall, her diary shows that she finally went to her doctor. For the next two and a half weeks, she continued to come to our house, except for five days when she came only half time. But on December 28, she was admitted to the hospital.

This period of illness is the only time in all of Grandma's journals from 1954 until 1985 that there are no entries. The silence runs from January 1 until April 15, 1962. On May 9, a simple entry states that she was discharged by her doctor.

It's not clear how long she was in the hospital, but one notation that's buried on a page in the back of her calendar suggests that it was a significant length of time. The note simply says, "January 30, 1962—Stopped compresses and dangled legs at side of bed for two periods of fifteen minutes." This implies that she was unable to care for herself, so it is quite likely that she was still in the hospital when she wrote that note about one month after being admitted to the hospital.

Could it be that she didn't write in her diary during her time of illness because it would have been all about her own medical situation? Most of her diary entries deal with what she did for others, or with others, and not with what was happening to her. Writing about her own condition would have been uncharacteristic, and her being unable to do anything while she was sick left little to say.

For the rest of Grandma's life, she was very careful not to let anyone come near her leg, for fear of it being re-injured. When I reflect on the three-inch wide, gaping hole, with only a thin, opaque piece of skin covering it, I'm reminded of what she did for us and what it cost her. But I wonder if she even thought about the cost.

# CHAPTER II

# A Voice Wrapped in Love

F OLLOWING MY PARENTS' long illness and Grandma's time in the hospital, there was a lot of turmoil on the home front. It had been less than a year since May of 1961, when my parents moved us to our own house. But I still longed to feel the comfort of Grandma's home, where I felt safe. In my parents' house, I didn't have that same assurance, and as I write this, something that happened when I was eleven years old screams out from the basement of my memory.

One particular day, my mother was resting in her bedroom, which was the first room along the hallway from the kitchen. She was feeling better after her bout with hepatitis, but being the two eldest, my sister and I still were expected to take care of a lot of the household duties. While I was making sandwiches at the kitchen counter next to the stove, a friend of my dad's came up beside me, stood close to my left, and put his arm firmly around my shoulders. I was trapped in the corner where the counter formed an "L" shape at the stove.

With his hot breath, the man whispered in my ear, reached up my dress, and forced his big, offensive fingers between my legs. When I pulled back, his grip became stronger and he pushed more, while trying to assure me that it was OK. Since I had nowhere to go, I began talking loudly, causing him to loosen his grip so I could free myself and run to my mother. But the man followed and stood in the doorway to her room.

"What's the matter?" Mom asked as I quickly sat on the bed and leaned against her.

I glanced toward the man in the doorway and then back at my mom. But I said nothing. When I didn't respond, Mom simply said that I had work to do and needed to finish making the sandwiches.

I don't know if the man followed me back to the kitchen or what happened after that. I don't even remember what the man looked like. I don't think I want to remember—or even need to.

Sometime following this incident, and shortly after my parents' recovery from hepatitis, I experienced what the doctors said was a nervous breakdown. I was not yet twelve years of age, and I remember lying on the bed and burying my head in a pillow, wishing that everything would stop. Even a small sound, like someone walking softly down the hall, was like the loud noise of a workman stomping his heavy boots on the wood floors of a big, empty room. A whisper was like someone shouting in my ear.

I was admitted to the hospital and placed in isolation, with strict instructions that I was to have absolutely no visitors—especially my family. While there, I remember being held down and consoled by two nurses as the doctor administered a spinal tap. To this day, I don't know why that was done.

After the procedure, I had to lie perfectly still for twenty-four hours. Visitors were not allowed to see or speak to me in any way, yet Grandma was somehow permitted to talk with me over an intercom that the hospital staff used. I remember lying flat and listening to her voice through the speaker on the wall above the head of my bed. Her comforting words and the assurance she gave as I lay still in my peaceful hospital room felt like pure love. She couldn't touch me with her hands or wrap her arms around me, but she could hold me tenderly with the sound of her voice.

Besides telling about what was going on at home, Grandma's diaries are filled with entries about world events, the various commitments she had, and what was happening in the lives of her friends and family.

On the larger world stage, Hurricane Frieda did her best to disrupt life on the west coast in October of 1962; US President John F. Kennedy was assassinated in November of 1963; an earthquake devastated Alaska on Good Friday, March 27, 1964; and a short notation on April 29, 1965, simply says, "Earth Tremor, 8:30 A.M."

During those same years, Grandma refers in her diaries to friends like Mrs. Irvine, who went to be with the Lord, and Paul Anhorn, who died when he fell down a flight of stairs. There also are significant entries that talk about staying with her friend Reta for extended periods of time, until she died on October 23, 1964.

She didn't seem to think twice about caring for family or friends who needed her help. And yet, while she did that, she also managed to keep her commitments to things like helping at the Children's Treatment Centre Fair, taking teacher training for Daily Vacation Bible School, attending various church-related committees and events, cooking at summer camp on the campus of what is now Trinity Western University, taking my sister and me shopping, and attending band concerts in which I performed.

Watching Grandma taught me a lot about friendship and love—even though I didn't realize it at the time. Her dedication to those she loved was sincere. And when they really needed help, she was there. Nothing seemed to be an inconvenience.

As I write this, I realize that her attitudes about friendship affect how I am today with my close friends, and I see my children and grandchildren being much the same way with their friends. It's interesting how that is. We mentor even when we don't realize it, and the effects are seen for generations.

Grandma (Mabel) and Granddaughter Ann (3 months), 1950

Grandma (Mabel) and Granddaughter
Ann (3), 1953

Sisters: Ann (4) and Pat (3), 1954

Siblings: Pat (5), Ann (6),
Bert (1 1/2), 1956

Ann (7) and her brother Ian (1), March
1958

All dressed up at Auntie Flora's. Ann (7), Grandma (Mabel), Bert (2 1/2), Ian
(3 months), Mom (Doreen), Pat (5), Summer 1957

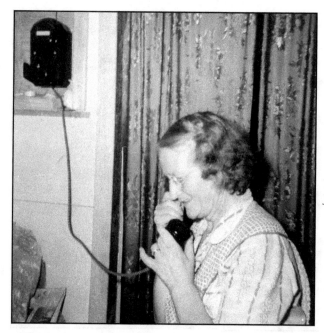

Grandma receives a rare phone call from her family in England, July 1958

Church friends. Grandma is in the long coat directly to the right of the post, 1958

# CHAPTER 12

# Girls Don't Play Drums

S OMEHOW I MADE it through my isolation illness and passed into grade seven—my senior year of elementary school. During the summer of 1962, before grade seven began, I met an older teenager who lived in our neighborhood and played bass drum in a marching band. I was intrigued and knew instinctively that I wanted to play the drums, never thinking that "girls don't play drums."

Lessons were out of the question, so I started going along with my friend to attend rehearsals of the Fireman's Junior Band at the local fire hall. Twice a week, the firemen drove the trucks out of the station so the teens and young adult members of the marching band could practice.

From the moment I strapped a snare drum to my slight, twelve-year-old, girlish frame and held a pair of sticks in my hands, it felt as if I was born to play. In no time at all, I learned how to play along with the rest of the band as we practiced songs by composers like John Phillip Sousa and modern tunes put to marching-style music.

In a few short weeks I was given my own uniform, and I began marching in parades, although I often was told that the drum looked as big as I was. I had discovered a deep love for music and rhythm, and the calendar that hung on the kitchen wall became riddled with practice and performance dates.

When school started in September, we were told that a high school music teacher would be coming once a week to work with grade seven students who were interested in learning to read music and play an instrument. Mr. Don Murray already had the reputation of being an exceptional teacher and award-winning conductor of concert bands, so this was considered a privilege. I jumped at the opportunity.

Grandma's calendars show that by December I was playing with the junior high concert band and, within a few short months, also was part of the senior band known as Surrey Schools' Concert Band. I was a lowly elementary school student who was playing with the high school kids and loving every minute of it. Music became the place where I felt a sense of worth, and the drums became my best friends.

By the time I turned thirteen and approached the end of grade seven, I was juggling school work, working in an after-school nanny job, rehearsing with three different bands, and practicing every minute I could. Church was also still a part of my life, as I continued to attend with Grandma and participate in Pioneer Girls club and Sunday school. Life was busy, and my own identity was emerging. But I don't think Grandma was always in favor of where she thought my new-found friends, busy life, and high school influences might lead me.

At this point in my life, I began to wrestle with right and wrong, good and bad, and black and white. While everyone seemed happy about my music involvement, my grandma's and parents' opinions were polar opposites on everything else. I felt pulled between the two.

On the one hand, Mom and Dad were happy about my playing the drums, and Mom even started a scrapbook of my concerts and performances for me to keep. They seemed genuinely proud of my accomplishments, but they were adamantly against my doing anything that involved church. They wanted me to spend time with kids who were sometimes doing things that I don't think my parents were aware of. And they pushed me to go to school dances, even though it felt wrong because none of the church kids were allowed to go.

On the other hand, Grandma was happy about my involvement in music, but she was concerned about some of the kids I associated with. She dropped strong hints that it would be better for me to spend more time with girls from church and encouraged me to stay involved with church activities.

I was living with my parents but still influenced by what Grandma thought. I didn't want to disappoint her. It was as if my parents sat on one of my shoulders, pulling or pushing me in one direction, while Grandma sat on the other, telling me that church was where I belonged.

As a budding teenager, I wanted to experience new things and devour all kinds of music—rock and roll, classical, military, pop, and the top hits on the radio, which included the controversial new music of the Beatles. I wanted to know how to play them all. But in the middle of my desire to experience music and explore new things, Grandma's voice rang consistently in my ear.

Taboos were loudly proclaimed by church people in general and gently reinforced by Grandma. Things like, "Nice Christian girls don't go to dances or movies." Or, "Good girls don't drink or smoke." Grandma would add, "You don't need make-up either. Look at how red my lips and cheeks are. I don't wear it."

I couldn't forget an experience I had when I was nine years old and my mom wouldn't write a note to release me from square dancing in gym class. A parent's note was the only way to get out of the class, and it usually was given for religious or health reasons. When I fell on the cement floor and broke my elbow during one of the classes, Grandma simply said, "It wouldn't have happened if she hadn't been dancing."

In most church circles, movies and dances were thought to be wrong, and though most people were supportive of my involvement in music, an unwritten rule said that drums did not belong in church. These restrictions may sound strange today, but the Christian community of the early sixties was different from what it is now. Right or wrong, what was once considered inappropriate, and even sinful, is not necessarily the way it is today.

At the time, I struggled to make sense of why God would give me a talent that contradicted what was considered acceptable in the church. Thankfully, that outlook changed, and I have used the gift God gave me to play in places and with people far beyond what I could have imagined as a young teenager.

# CHAPTER 13

# Maybe I *Can* Write

WHEN MY MOM left my dad in 1956, my sister and I only had one brother, Bert. A few months after that event, in 1957, another brother, Ian, was born. After Mom and Dad got back together and Dad joined us at Grandma's in 1959, Keith, brother number three, came home from the hospital. By the time we moved from Grandma's in 1961, her home was bursting with five children between the ages of two and eleven years old. And there were more children to come.

Two weeks before I entered junior high school in 1963, my brother Michael (Eric) was born, followed thirteen months later, in the fall of 1964, by my youngest brother, David. During what felt like a chaotic period, key events occurred that changed the course of my life—events in which Grandma continued to play a major role.

In the summer of 1964, I attended the Canadian Sunday School Mission's Hope Bay Bible Camp, which is located on Pender Island, off the coast of British Columbia, Canada. Knowing how my parents felt about church-related activities, I'm not sure how I got there or who paid for it, but it changed my life. It seems to have been significant to Grandma as well, because even though she noted my departure and return from Pioneer Girl Camp and Camp Artaban in two previous years, her entry on August 7, 1964, proclaims, "Ann home from a happy camp."

On my way to camp at Hope Bay, I didn't feel very confident. I excelled in music but struggled deeply with low self-image. My report cards consistently said, "Ann is conscientious and hardworking," but my grades didn't show it. I was skinny, felt unattractive in clothes that seemed to hang on me, and was developing physically at a slower rate than the other girls at school. Even though I felt great when I played the drums, I wasn't really sure where I belonged. At camp I thought a lot about these things and about my grandma, who was always there for me. She loved me unconditionally, and the letter I wrote to her from my camp cot reflects how much I loved her.

It was at camp that I questioned where God fit into my life and everything that surrounded it. Despite the fact that I attended Sunday school, memorized Bible verses, and argued with my parents, trying to get them to let me attend events at church, I realized that I had been doing a lot of it for Grandma. When I became aware of how important it was for me to have my own personal relationship with God, I made the decision to accept Him as Savior and Lord of my life. With my camp counselor, I prayed and then made that commitment public.

Before the end of the week, I used bright and bold shades of red and blue to paint a plaster plaque that read, "God Loves Me." When camp was over, I left with plaque in hand and the solid assurance that God cared about me. No matter how much upheaval there was in my life or what I would face in the future, I knew that He was there in the middle of it all—holding me tightly.

When I returned home, I was passionate about my relationship with God and read my Bible faithfully, sometimes hiding under the blankets with a flashlight so my parents wouldn't get angry. I became involved in the leadership of Inter-School Christian Fellowship and the church youth group and kept a full schedule of music, which was still a major part of my life.

At fourteen years of age, I had decided that I wanted to live my life for God. But while Grandma was delighted and supportive of my decision, the gulf between my parents and me grew.

This was also the point in my life when I began writing bits of poetry. For fun, I sometimes put new words to popular tunes that I liked. It was a great way to combine words with music that expressed my feelings. And it helped me to learn the value of rhythm in songs and poetry.

One day, I was especially happy with the words I'd written to a familiar song, and I proudly gave it to my mom to look over. After a quick read, she handed the paper back to me and said, "You can't write words to someone else's music."

I had discovered that I loved words, but my mother's words cut like a knife through the fledgling writer within me. From that day forward, I second-guessed almost everything I wrote that others would see. But I secretly continued to jot down random thoughts and bits of poetry for myself.

In my senior year of high school, the school counselor saw one of my poems, recommended it to the yearbook committee, and prompted me to write more. It was then that I began to think, *Maybe I can write.* And yet, throughout my life, the joy I felt when I wrote was haunted by the memory of my mother's words and the question: what if I write something wrong?

## Personal Reflection

1. What memory or decision affected your life, even though you may not have realized it at the time? How did it affect your life? How does it affect you today?

2. Where did you feel safe as a child? How can you create that feeling of safety for your grandchildren/family?

3. When did you realize that God loves you? How can you demonstrate God's love to your grandchildren?

4. What special ability did you exhibit when you were younger but set aside because of other people's needs, expectations, or demands?

5. As your grandchildren volunteer at summer camp, at church, or in the community, how can you support/encourage/bless them in their venture?

# CHAPTER 14

# Silence Runs Deep

L EADING UP TO April of 1965, Grandma's diaries are filled with commitments to do housework for other people, care for sick friends, attend funerals, and fulfill responsibilities at church and in the community. Then on April 13, her diary reads, "Had quarrel with Doreen." Except for one incident that I'm aware of, the silence between Grandma and my mom remained until exactly the same day the following year, when Grandma's diary says, "Doreen spoke to me."

Though I never was told what the disagreement with my mother, Grandma's only child, was about, I remember that year well. While Grandma avoided talking with me about the issue, my parents, with whom I was living at the time, often referred to Grandma in non-flattering and derogatory terms. Each time I heard them, I felt anger and pain. What they said didn't measure up to the grandma I knew. But despite their words, my relationship with Grandma grew stronger.

When possible, I spent weekends at Grandma's or went shopping with her. In those days, there weren't a lot of stores in Surrey, where we lived, so Grandma and I boarded the bus in the morning and crossed the Patullo Bridge to the main bus depot in New Westminster. From there, we walked five blocks down the steep Sixth Street hill to Columbia Street, where many people went to shop. Halfway down the hill, we always stopped at the Bible book store. I loved to look at all the different books while Grandma chatted with the owner of the store and purchased the small New Testaments that she gave to any new baby that was born to a family in our church.

After we made our way down the rest of the hill, we walked up and down Columbia Street, going in and out of stores to find the things on Grandma's list. If it was the time of year when Grandma took me shopping for my birthday present, we stopped at every clothing store to find just the right outfit—usually a dress. But because I couldn't make up my mind which outfit I liked best, we invariably ended our shopping day back at the first store where I had tried something on. Despite my indecision, Grandma never showed impatience.

At lunch time, we stopped at Kresge's lunch counter for a rest and something to eat. When we were finished for the day, we retraced our steps up the hill to catch the bus back to Surrey and walk the final blocks home from the bus stop.

Now, as an adult, when I drive along the steep Sixth Street hill, I think about those trips and how it must have been an effort for Grandma. But she never complained and always made it a special day for the two of us.

Weekend stays at Grandma's were wonderful because they felt familiar and comfortable. We did things like sort through old trunks, where treasures and photos gave me a deeper glimpse into Grandma's younger life. Or we worked in the garden, and she told me about how she and Grandpa cleared the land by hand when they purchased the tree-covered property. Or we talked about the many fruit trees she planted after his death—apple, cherry, plum, and pear. Some of them still were bearing fruit.

The funniest part of those stories was imagining my proper English grandma, whom I never saw wear anything but dresses, sporting overalls and working one end of a buck saw that required two people to operate. One photo shows Grandma on one end of the saw, with Grandpa Imerson on the other. They were pushing and pulling the saw through the trunk of a large tree before it gave way to their efforts and fell to the ground. Another photo shows the two of them sitting on a large stump with their arms around each other. They looked so happy.

By the summer of 1965, life at my parents' house had become very difficult for me, and I wanted out. When I heard that a couple with four children was looking for a live-in nanny, I decided that was something I could do. After all, I just had turned fifteen years old and was the eldest in a household of seven children. Four couldn't be that hard to manage.

We knew the family, so when I heard about the job, I met with the mother of the children. Soon an agreement was struck. The little money I earned over my room and board was to take care of the coming year's school expenses and pay for the extracurricular band activities I was involved in. The family lived halfway between my parents' house and Grandma's home, so I was still in the neighborhood and able to see Grandma and attend church.

When I moved in with the family who employed me, I was given a small room with a single bed and dresser. I had never had my own room, so I felt like I was in heaven. But it soon became clear to me that the job I had taken on was not heavenly.

The three boys, who were about twelve, ten, and eight years old, and one girl, who was about six, were unruly, disobedient, and always seemed to be fighting with each other. I was accustomed to hearing extremely foul language from my truck-driver father, but when I consistently heard it from the mouth of the ten-year-old boy, I wasn't sure how to handle it. Nothing I said or did seemed to make a difference.

As the summer came to a close, the thought of returning to my parents' house was less appealing to me than the work situation I was in, although that wasn't ideal either. To avoid having to go back to my parents, I arranged to stay on as nanny to the four children, with the understanding that I would be able to continue school.

Each morning, I helped get the children ready for school and then walked about a mile and a half to the local junior high school, where I was a grade ten student. In those days, elementary school went from grade one through grade seven, junior high school covered grades eight through ten, and high school was for grades eleven and twelve. At the end of classes, I walked back to my job, arriving in time to get the children their after-school snack and begin making dinner.

It was during that fall that the school counselor and principal talked with my mother about moving me from the school's academic track that prepared students for university to the general track that prepared students to enter a trade school or join the labor workforce. To me, this was a real blow because it said that there was no way I would be able to study music at university and pursue the career I thought I wanted.

At that time, the school ran on a division system. The more academically inclined students were in the lower numbered divisions, and the higher divisions were for students who were not likely to go on in school. For example, Division One was made up of the kids whom everyone saw as "the smart kids," those who would go on to great things. Students in the higher numbered divisions were taught skills and some basic academics so they could get by in the real world.

As if being told I wasn't good enough to prepare for university wasn't bad enough, I was assigned to Division 15—the highest number division in the general program. The only level with a higher division number than fifteen was the occupational class that was reserved for students who were considered to have academic deficiencies.

Being labeled as "one of the dumb kids"—even if it was only in my mind—didn't help the self-image issues I already was dealing with. But instead of defeating me, it seemed to ignite a fire in me. No matter where they put me, I was determined to prove myself.

All through that year, band was the one place in school where I excelled and felt seen and accepted. Teachers and students acknowledged my talent. Mr. Murray assigned drum solos for me to perform at concerts, gave me public accolades, taught me how to conduct the band, and had me learn to play other instruments, like trumpet, saxophone, and French horn. In my mind, he was telling me I had worth. Whether or not he realized the significance of his actions, he encouraged and challenged me to pursue the gift God had given me. He made a positive, long-term difference in my life.

Two months into that fall, it became evident that the pace I was keeping and the demands I was putting on myself were too much. Something had to change, and it seemed logical that it was the nanny job that had to go. But that also meant I had to move—and I still didn't want to go back to my parents' house.

When I talked with Grandma about it, she was more than happy to have me move in with her, but she said I had to check with my parents first.

"Mom, I can't keep going to school and working as a nanny, so I'm quitting the nanny job. Is it OK if I go live with Grandma?" I asked.

"I don't know. Go ask your father," she replied.

"Dad, I can't keep going to school and working as a nanny, so I'm quitting the nanny job. Is it OK if I move in with Grandma?" I asked.

"I don't know. Go ask your mother," he replied.

"But Mom told me to talk to you."

"Well, I don't know. It's her mother. Talk to her."

"Mom, Dad said I'm supposed to talk with you about moving in with Grandma."

"I don't know, Ann. Your father and I will have to talk about it."

By the end of the first week of November of 1965, I still didn't have the answer to my question, although I'm not sure what I expected. After all, Grandma and my parents hadn't spoken to each other since April. I was afraid to keep asking, for fear that they'd say "no," but I decided to try again.

"Mom, my job is finished, and I need to move. What did you and Dad decide about my going to live with Grandma?" I persisted.

"We haven't talked about it."

"But I need an answer," I explained.

By Wednesday, November 10, I still had not received their answer, but I had to move. After school that day, I packed my few belongings and walked to Grandma's. I was finally home—really home. But for how long?

# CHAPTER 15

# Call in the Night

W HEN I ARRIVED home from school, Grandma was usually in the kitchen baking, finishing an ironing or a sewing job for someone, or preparing for a meeting of the Women's Missionary Society or another group or committee she was involved with. The house was peaceful and quiet; the only sound was the music coming from the radio on her kitchen table.

After dropping my books and hanging up my coat, we sat together over tea and a snack and talked about the day. If Grandma was away working at someone's house, I had something quick to eat and did my homework before she arrived home for dinner.

In the evening, I went to band rehearsals or youth group commitments, and Grandma watched her black-and-white TV while knitting, crocheting, or working on a crossword puzzle—unless she too had a meeting to attend. On evenings when neither of us had to be out, we read or watched TV together and talked. She was rarely idle and never watched TV without doing something with her hands at the same time.

Because Grandma was a masterful seamstress and creator of beautiful knitted or crocheted outfits, people often hired her to make sweaters or baby outfits. In addition to the details of the jobs she undertook, whom she worked for, how long she worked each day, and how much she earned, her records from the 1930s, 40s, and 50s listed the names of people she knitted and crocheted for and what she was paid for each piece. Buried between the pages of the record books, she also saved a blue three-by-five award card that said:

**HJORTH ROAD GARDEN CLUB**
**Eighth Annual Show**
August 17th, 1946
**FIRST PRIZE**
Awarded to: Mrs. Imerson
Article: Knitted socks

As my siblings and I grew and had babies of our own, Grandma knitted beautiful shawls for each of them. Not long ago, my young granddaughter Calista proudly showed me a carefully wrapped package that she had stored among her keepsakes in her room. The package contained two sweater outfits my grandma had made for Calista's daddy when he was a little boy. To her, they were treasures. For me, they held priceless memories.

In addition to the daily demands of caring for her own household, Grandma's schedule often was filled with church and community meetings. She also made extra income by doing odd jobs, like cleaning, ironing, sewing, painting, gardening, and even mending fish nets. Most of my time was taken up with school work, youth group activities, band rehearsals or performances, and household chores. To help out, I also earned money by babysitting neighbor children and teaching drums to a couple of young boys. The money I earned was carefully stored in my secret hiding place—the bedpost of Grandma's brass bed.

On weekends, Grandma wrote letters to her family in England and to missionaries around the world. We also worked together on household projects, and she occasionally took me to visit her elderly friends. It wasn't until years later that I realized those visits had given me a different kind of education—one that taught me valuable lessons on friendship, showed me a different side of my grandma, and instilled in me a respect for elderly people. Grandma had learned to be content when she was on her own, but she also loved being with people and doing things for them.

While I knew that Grandma went to the homes of friends to help with things they couldn't physically do for themselves, it was during our visits that I saw how much she cared about them personally. She seemed to bring a calm energy that encouraged them as we chatted over tea or a meal. And it was clear to me that they too enjoyed their relationship with Grandma.

On those occasions, I listened to what was happening in their lives at the time and to the stories of their earlier days. Yet, though I heard my grandma laugh with her friends, she often seemed to have some tentativeness about her that I could not explain. It was as if she carried a shield or wore a suit of armor. Was she protecting herself? If so, from what? Or was it my imagination?

Grandma enjoyed visiting with friends in their homes, but she rarely had them to her house for tea—and never for a meal. When she did have friends in, it was because they invited themselves or spontaneously dropped by. It was as if she was self-conscious about her humble home that didn't measure up to most other homes of the day. And she was well aware of her overgrown yard that was too much for her to take care of.

I also noticed that she avoided conversations about my mom and family. If someone asked questions about my parents, she only gave brief answers. Though she always made me feel that she was proud of me, I can't help but wonder if she was embarrassed about her overall family situation and the way her life had turned out. Did she feel that she hadn't achieved her dreams for her life? Or that she hadn't accomplished what her parents and siblings expected when she left them to get married in the land of opportunity those many years before? Then again, maybe that's just speculation on my part.

As I now reflect back, using my adult perspective, I think I understand a little of what she was protecting herself from. Or do I? Maybe it was about something altogether different. Maybe it was a secret she chose to keep buried deep within herself. Maybe… Maybe…Maybe…

No matter what might have been the cause of the tentativeness or shield that I detected, Grandma always seemed to approach life with courage and a positive, can-do attitude that said her cup was half full—not half empty.

I don't recall ever hearing Grandma enter into a conversation that could lead to conflict. Yet I knew from my childhood experiences that she took a stand when it came to something or someone she strongly believed in. She had opinions and told me her thoughts on certain issues when I pressed her, but when it came to other people, she usually avoided controversy.

I wonder if she stayed away from those discussions because her family life was filled with enough sadness and conflict and she was protecting herself. Or maybe she chose to focus only on what she saw as important. Or perhaps she just was living up to her name—Nancy means grace, and Mabel means lovable.

For the six weeks after I moved in with Grandma, I enjoyed the sanctuary of her home—my home—our home. Our life together was full and wonderful. But on Tuesday, December 21, 1965, one phone call changed everything that was wonderful.

A loud ring sounded from across the room. Grandma, in her usual fashion, jumped up and rushed to where the black phone was mounted on the wall. When she got her first phone installed on December 29, 1952, she had a cubbyhole cut into the wall especially for the phone. Lifting the receiver from its cradle, she said, "Hello."

Within a few short words, her demeanor cooled, and I realized she was talking with my mom. They hadn't spoken since April, but as I listened, Grandma's short responses gave me the impression that this was a one-sided conversation—and not a pleasant social one. I had no idea what the call was about, but I could tell it had something to do with me.

Finally, Grandma removed the phone from her ear and covered the mouthpiece with her hand. "Ann, your mother insists that you go back to their place," she said quietly.

"But I don't want to go back. I want to stay with you," I replied as I got up from the couch and walked toward her.

"I know," she replied sadly. "I want you here; but she says that if you don't go back right away, she will call the authorities and they will come take you away."

"Can they do that?" I asked.

"I'm not sure what they can do, but I know that she will call them. It's the kind of thing she would do."

I felt like a tiny rabbit cornered by a big barking dog. "Grandma, what can we do?" I asked. "I don't want to go back."

"I'm sorry, but this time I think you need to go," she replied. "Your mother will do what she says she will do. And I don't know what that might mean. It could make things very bad for you. Don't worry; I'm still here. But for now, I think it's best that you do what she says."

Grandma was right. For now, there seemed to be no other choice. I had to go back to my parents—even though neither of us liked it.

"All right," Grandma said into the phone. "It's late now, so Ann will come tomorrow."

After hanging up the phone, she walked across the room to where I had made my way back to the couch. Together we sat in silence.

# CHAPTER 16

# The Reluctant Return

THE NEXT DAY, I packed a few of my belongings and trudged along the same road I had walked four years before, when I first left Grandma's home. Then it was July, flowers were blooming, and I was eleven years old. This time, it was December, snow was falling, and I was fifteen.

Exactly six weeks had passed since I had moved back to Grandma's. Now that I was leaving again, I knew they could take me away from her physically, but they could not erase the love and respect I had for her.

Back in my parents' house, it didn't take long for me to be reminded that my mom and dad didn't agree on much of anything, although they did see eye-to-eye on one thing—me. They made it very clear that they did not want me to spend time with Grandma or be involved in anything to do with church. But whether it was out of pure stubbornness or a belief that I must go, I stood firm. As much as possible, I went to church and youth group, where I had become part of the committee of young people who gave leadership to the church youth.

Between music and church activities, my schedule became so busy that I think my parents were often not sure where I was going or what I was doing. On Sunday mornings, they usually got up late, so I left for church while they slept. For evening events, I simply expected to go and arranged for someone to pick me up. When my ride arrived, I said a quick "good-bye" and left.

To my young mind, I was standing up for what I believed. But I struggled to reconcile my own life experiences with the verse in the Bible that says, "Honor your father and mother . . ." I didn't feel loved or respected by my parents, and they didn't appear to honor their parents. I reasoned that God wouldn't expect me to honor parents who questioned or denied His existence and who told me to do what I saw as contrary to God's Word. Or would He?

Whether I was returning from a church youth event or a band rehearsal, I dreaded going home at night. It seemed that my dad almost always was drinking and my mom usually was talking on the phone or upset about something.

To enter the house, we didn't use the front door that usually was blocked by boxes or a piece of furniture. Instead, we walked through the carport, up four stairs to a four-by-six-foot landing and came in by the back door. Once in the house, we walked through the laundry room to the kitchen.

Finding our way through the laundry room was like maneuvering a maze or obstacle course. The first hurdle was a Doberman dog named Whiskey, who often was scratching himself and complained when he was rousted from his spot on the outside step or just inside the door. When we made it inside, we had to choose carefully where to step on the gritty plywood floor, while a myriad of smells assaulted our senses—the powerful odors of wet dog, piles of stinking laundry that hopelessly waited to be washed, and the overpowering stench of sweat-ridden shoes and socks that my mom used to say could stand in the corner by themselves. With no door separating the laundry room from the rest of the house, the offensive smells merged with the gas fumes from the stove in the kitchen and flowed to the rest of the house.

Once through the laundry room maze, we entered the kitchen. Just inside and to the right stood a white fridge that was piled high with dust-covered papers and items that threatened to collide with the cupboard above. Next to the fridge was a propane stove with a stick propped against the oven door to keep it closed and an aluminum pot of tea that simmered on top of the stove all day. To the left of the entrance to the kitchen was an archway that led into the hallway to the bedrooms. Straight ahead was Control Central, where Dad sat an arm's length away from whoever passed by.

Four years had elapsed since we moved into the new house, yet the walls still were covered in the same unpainted and not-yet-taped sheetrock. The bare plywood countertops and open cupboards remained the same, except for the accumulation of dirt, grime, grease, and cigarette smoke that now enveloped the floors, cupboards, and walls.

My parents' impatience and subsequent anger towards me had increased since I moved back from Grandma's, which meant that I never knew what to expect when I walked into the house.

One night when I came home, Dad was sitting at his usual place in the kitchen at the end of the big weathered oak table, and Mom sat across from him. My heart pounded when I entered the kitchen, and I stayed as close as possible to the fridge, so as to avoid contact with my dad. He never had struck me, but he had grabbed me with his strong hands, and he had hit my brothers. Also, in a fit of anger, he once had put his fist through the wall behind his chair at the kitchen table and thrown one of my brothers down the hall. I wasn't taking any chances.

Making my way past the fridge and my dad, I stepped up to the kitchen counter to make my lunch for the next day of school. While I tried to be invisible, I could hear my parents talking behind me.

The table where they sat was positioned along a twelve-foot wall that ran from one end of the kitchen, where my dad sat, to the other end, which flowed into the dining room. At the dining room end of the wall was a wider doorway, like an arch, that divided the dining room from the living room. The configuration made it possible for the younger children to pretend they were running around a racetrack—moving from the kitchen to the dining room, on through the living room, and back into the kitchen. Of course, that only happened when Dad wasn't there.

While the wall with archways at both ends separated the kitchen from the living room, a section of counter separated the kitchen from the dining room that opened into the living room. The counter never was used for cooking because it almost always was covered with mounds of papers and anything else that found its way there. The open dining room was more like a storage room that held two large freezers and numerous tattered boxes. It also was the place where Dad kept his own still for making homemade beer and dandelion wine and a couple of crocks with fermenting cabbage destined to be sauerkraut. The foul odors that emanated from the souring cabbage and aging hops added to the other smells of the house. When the beer or wine was ready for bottling, my sister and I had to help.

When I entered the kitchen, I had to pass my dad, who sat by the doorway that led to the hall and bedrooms. However, once I was in the kitchen, there was an alternate way to get to my bedroom without walking back past him. My plan was to finish making my school lunch and move quickly from the kitchen, through the dining room and living room, and on down the hallway to my room. I reasoned that if Dad really wanted to get hold of me, he'd have to get up from his chair and step into the hall.

That night, my parents were in especially foul moods, and they began listing all the things about me that upset them. I tried to stay focused on making my school lunch and not respond or make eye contact, but they seemed to take my non-response as a show of defiance and disrespect. Their accusations hurt deeply, and I felt my face get hot as their voices escalated. Dad cursed, and they both spoke negatively about Grandma and accused me of thinking I was better than everyone else. I wanted to fight back. And I wanted to run.

Before turning to leave the room, I faced my accusers and made a lame attempt at defending Grandma. Mom railed on about how they were my parents and I was supposed to do as I was told. Dad's steely-blue, bloodshot eyes glared with rage as he affirmed, "You listen to your mother."

I knew it was time to exit the room—*now*.

# CHAPTER 17

# The Lost Is Found

FOR THE NEXT six months, I immersed myself in school, music, and church youth activities, taking advantage of every opportunity to be away from home. At my parents' house, I felt tension and fear, but at Grandma's, I felt love and acceptance. She made a world of difference in my life.

During this time, Grandma was busy, but not too busy to spend time with me. Each weekday, the mile-and-a-half trek from school took me past her house. It was set back from the road on two-and-a-half acres of land. For economic survival, she'd had to sell half of the original five acres after Grandpa Imerson died. The driveway that ran from the road to her home was long, and she didn't like my having to walk it if she wasn't home. To remedy this, she devised a signal I could see from the road. When she was home, she put an eight-inch by ten-inch piece of white cardboard in the window facing the road. If the paper was there, I knew she was home. If it wasn't there, I knew she wasn't home. On the days the paper wasn't in the window, I remember being disappointed as I continued on to my parents' house. On the days she was home, I happily made my way up the driveway for a visit.

I often was wet and cold when I arrived because it seemed to snow or rain during most of the school year, and I didn't have a pair of boots. Grandma still didn't have central heating in her house, so I went straight to the kitchen and sat by the open oven door of the oil stove. If my feet were really cold, Grandma cautioned me not to get too close to the heat. But even though my feet sometimes hurt as they warmed and life returned to them, being in her home felt good.

The after-school visits with Grandma were wonderful. While my shoes and coat dried and I warmed up, Grandma made me tea and toast with jelly or brown sugar and cinnamon and a cup of instant coffee for herself. And we talked. She asked me how I was doing at school, how things were going at home or in other areas of my life, and filled me in on her latest activities. Sometimes I asked her about snippets of memories I recalled from my childhood, and she answered my questions as best she could.

On one occasion, I told her about a dream I'd been having and the thoughts I couldn't get out of my mind. "Grandma, I dream the same dream over and over. There's always a baby in it, and I can't seem to get the baby out of my mind. It's as if this baby is supposed to mean something to me—but I don't know why."

Grandma sat and listened but didn't offer an explanation.

Finally, I asked, "Was there another baby in our family when I was younger?"

Lifting her cup to her lips, she took a sip of coffee, closed her eyes, and leaned back in her chair. I sat quietly, waiting. When she opened her eyes, she looked at me and simply said, "Yes."

"Yes?" I asked.

"I guess you're old enough to understand," she replied and went on to explain. "When you all came with your mom to live here with me, she was expecting a baby. Seven months later, your brother Ian was born. Thirteen months after his birth, another baby boy was born, on May 9, 1958. Your parents were still apart, and another child meant that there would be five children to support. They were very difficult years in many ways, so the baby was put up for adoption."

"Did the baby ever live here with us? What was his name? What happened to him?" I asked.

"He was adopted from the hospital, but I don't know what happened to him after that," she replied.

That was the end of the conversation. We never again talked about the baby, and I didn't tell my mother what I had learned. Many years later, my eldest niece, Susette, heard about the skeleton in our family closet and set out to find our lost brother—her uncle.

Shortly after she began her search, Susette learned that the government required my mom's signed approval to proceed. However, because it wasn't known how the news would affect Mom or Dad, it was decided to put the search on hold.

After the passing of my father on September 25, 1991, my sister and niece told Mom about the initial search for our lost brother and the roadblock they had encountered. She gave her approval and the search was renewed.

Not long after she signed the necessary papers, Mom received a call from the authorities, saying that our lost brother had been found and that he too wanted to find us. After the initial meeting between my mom and her son, arrangements were made for a sibling reunion that took place on March 1, 1997—thirty-nine years after the adoption.

Following the successful reunion, unanswered questions lingered in my mind, but Mom didn't seem too willing to answer them—because she couldn't remember, chose to avoid them, or didn't want to talk about it. Grandma had passed away by this time, and there was no one left to ask, except one woman.

Ivy Anhorn had been a close neighbor friend to Grandma and our family, and I believed she was the only one who knew parts of the story Grandma hadn't told me. The two of us met at a local restaurant and sipped on cups of coffee while Ivy satisfied my curiosity and revealed the role Grandma had played in the situation.

"By the middle of 1958, your grandma had had your mom and you kids living in her home for almost two years, and she had pretty well supported all of you," Ivy explained. "When your mom announced that she was expecting another child, it was already hard to provide for all of you. With no father in the picture and so much uncertainty, Grandma believed that the baby would have a better chance at life if he was adopted by a family who would love him, provide for him, and raise him in a much better home environment. Her decision to insist that your mom put the baby up for adoption was because she wanted him to have a better life. She felt it would be best for him and for the rest of you kids. And, as you know, it seems that she was right."

More questions. More listening. And Ivy continued.

"When the baby was born, the hospital required a name for their records and to register the birth. But a name had not been chosen for him. While we stood in the hospital, I said the first name that came to my mind, and that's what stuck."

The name, Gregory Worrall, was written on the Registration of Birth form, and he went to live with his new family, who changed his name to Trevor. I don't know if they knew that our dad's name was Trevor or that Dad wasn't with our family. But I assume they were aware of some of the circumstances surrounding the birth of this fifth child. When I talked with Trevor's adoptive mom at the sibling reunion, she told me that they chose the name Trevor because they liked it. And Gregory Worrall became Trevor Wesley Peters.

Did Grandma give Mom an ultimatum when she insisted that the baby be put up for adoption? I don't know. Did Mom willingly give up her fifth child, or did she fight to keep him? I don't know.

I can understand what it was like for Grandma to look at her grandchildren and want more for them than what they were receiving. I can speculate what it was like to insist that one of them be put up for adoption—for his good and for the good of all the children. On the other hand, I only can imagine what it was like to give up a baby and how it might have affected the relationship between my grandma and my mother.

Except for what I learned from others, I have no memory of the months or the struggles that my grandma and mom experienced around the birth and adoption of my little brother Trevor. Seven days before his birth in 1958, I turned eight years old. Today, the lost has been found, and we all enjoy being part of each other's lives.

## Personal Reflection

1. Mentally take a walk through your childhood home. What memories do you need to nurture? What memories do you need to let go of? What difference will that nurturing or letting go make in your life? What difference will that make in the life of your family?

2. What relationship has been broken in your family? What difference could healing that relationship make to you personally? How will that healing affect who you are as a grandparent? What could you do to help bring healing to that broken relationship? What will you do and by when?

3. What are you avoiding in your life that may negatively affect your relationships with family or friends? How do you think your grandchildren are affected by it?

4. What did you learn about relationships from your grandma and/or grandpa?

5. What are your grandchildren learning when they see you with your friends and family? What would you like them to learn from your relationships with others? What do you need to change so this can happen?

6. How do you create opportunities for conversation with your grandchildren?

# CHAPTER 18

# At the Movies

A S THE 1965–66 school year came to a close, I couldn't imagine spending a whole summer at my parents' house. One day in June of 1966, a couple who knew my parents and my grandma made it known that they were looking for a live-in nanny for their two girls, who were five and six years old. The family lived in a house that Mr. Dainard built on the property of the drive-in theater they owned and operated and where they also kept a few head of cattle. The summer job required that I help around the house in the daytime and look after the girls at night while Mrs. Dainard managed the concession stand and Mr. Dainard ran the movie projectors at the theater. In addition to the two daughters, Mr. and Mrs. Dainard had three grown sons, who all lived away from home and were a number of years older than their younger sisters.

Once everyone agreed on the work arrangement, I was delivered to the Dainards' home, which was ten miles from where we lived. When I stepped into the sixties-style, split-level house that felt like a mansion to me, my eyes fell on everything beautiful. A magnificent stone fireplace covered one full wall of the tastefully furnished living room; a richly polished wood table and ornate matching chairs with white, cloth-padded seats stood in the dining room; and the kitchen was bright, with lots of windows. On the lower level of the house was a play area and laundry room, and upstairs, there were bedrooms for everyone. The air smelled fresh and clean. And everything had its place.

When I was shown to my own room, it was like nothing I'd ever seen. It was bright and cheerful, with a double bed and furnishings just for me. Instead of wood or plaster, the far wall was a large picture window that looked out on the massive outdoor theater screen. In addition to being able to see the movies, I also could hear them through the room's privately-controlled sound system. I never had been to a movie theater before. Now I had a front-row seat to watch movies every night, if I wanted, and all from the comfort of my own room.

Each night, the girls' parents told me whether or not the movie was suitable for them to watch. If it was, the three of us curled up on my bed and watched the first movie together. If it wasn't, I did something else with them. By the time the next feature started, the girls were off to their own beds to sleep, and I was able to choose whether or not I wanted to watch the second movie or pull the drapes and go to sleep.

When extra help was needed at the snack bar between the two feature movies, the girls and I walked from the house to the center of the drive-in theatre grounds where there was a building that housed the concession stand, projection room, and public washrooms. While the girls visited their dad and he prepared the next movie reel, I learned how to take customers' orders, fill food orders, and give change for purchases.

During that summer, Mrs. Dainard took me under her wing. Besides teaching me how to clean her beautiful furniture, set a table properly with all the cutlery and glassware positioned just right, and serve customers in the concession stand, she also talked to me about life. She was aware of my family situation and took an interest in me. In retrospect, I realize that she mentored me. She made a difference in my life. I will be forever grateful for those two short months with her.

At the end of the summer, Mr. and Mrs. Dainard offered to let me stay with them while I attended school. If I chose to stay, I'd have to change high schools because they lived out of the catchment area, or boundary lines, of my current school. The problem with that was that the school in their area did not offer band classes, and music was a very important part of my life.

If I stayed, I felt that I'd have to forfeit going to university to study music, something I still dreamed about despite having already been transferred from the academic university track to the general program at school. I also would have to make new friends, and the move would take me away from my activities at church. On the other hand, staying would mean that I could continue to enjoy the wonderful living environment I had enjoyed all summer.

If I didn't stay, I could pursue my music, resume my church involvement after a summer away, and be nearer to Grandma. But where would I live? Though I didn't realize it at the time, this was a major crossroad in my life, and Grandma played a significant role.

After sorting through my choices and talking them over with Grandma and Mrs. Dainard, I knew I had to leave the Dainards' and go back to the school where I already was registered. I also knew that I didn't want to go back to my parents' house.

As my time at the Dainards' came to a close, I put my young faith to the test and prayed that God would work it out for me to move in with Grandma.

Once again, I approached my mother, with the clear memory of her response less than a year before when I had made a similar request. "Mom, I know this didn't work out before, but I really want to move in with Grandma. May I go live with her?"

To my surprise, she came right back with, "Yes."

I never asked why she and Dad had a change of heart; I just accepted her answer and moved into action. When I later heard her talk with her friends about my move, she said that Grandma was getting on in years and it probably wasn't good for her to live on her own in "that house."

I had no idea where she got that idea, but I didn't argue the point. It didn't matter how she came to her conclusion. When I told Grandma about it, she chuckled. She was still a very active sixty-seven-year-old. As for me, it strengthened my faith.

CHAPTER 19

# New Horizons to Discover

O N LABOR DAY, September 5, 1966, I said "good-bye" to the Dainards and moved in with Grandma. The next day, I started high school. I was sixteen years old and in grade eleven.

Over the next two years, I explored my leadership skills, challenged academic boundaries, defied the expectations of some authority figures in my life, experienced the triumph of musical achievement, and met the sailor who would change my life. It was a time to test my wings—and soar. Yet in retrospect, I'm not sure that would have happened without the love, support, freedom, and discipline I received while living in the security of Grandma's home.

High school was a growing time—a time when I discovered that I enjoyed being in leadership roles and organizing anything that needed to be organized. Church was the primary place where I tested those waters and where I was blessed to have people who encouraged and challenged me along the way.

Our church youth group was made up of teens who were thirteen years of age, or entering grade eight, on up to about eighteen years old, or beginning college. In those days, churches didn't have youth pastors. Instead, the young people themselves elected a peer leadership team that was responsible for holding weekly meetings, planning special events, and providing leadership to the youth program of the church. In addition, designated individuals from our congregation volunteered as youth sponsors and provided guidance and supervision to the youth leadership team.

Our main sponsor was a wonderful man whom we all knew simply as Mick. Mick McLellan sat in on our leadership team meetings and general youth gatherings, gave feedback on our ideas, and often went with us to events held away from the church. He was a gentle, reasonable, and godly man who loved young people and along with his wife, Peg, always opened his home to us. Mick also taught a Sunday school class at our church for high school and college students, who flocked to sit under his teaching.

For some of us older teens who wanted to dig deeper into the Bible, Mick led an evening Bible study in his home during the week. I have great memories of sitting on the living room floor of the McLellan home and studying the book of Romans with friends. Mick made this book of the Bible come alive and encouraged us to debate and ask questions. He also taught us how to use the Bible and other reference materials to find the answers for ourselves.

Our youth group's leadership team was generally made up of high school or first-year college students. They each had specific responsibilities and worked with their own subcommittees. Each subcommittee was then made up of other high school kids and younger teens who wanted to be involved. During my early teen years, I served on subcommittees, and as I grew older, I became more and more involved. By the time I was sixteen and in high school, I was elected president of the youth group. I loved this role and learned so much from those who mentored me over the next two years. I also learned by being willing to do whatever needed to be done—something I had watched Grandma do all my life.

In the spring of 1967, Van and Pat Neudorf, who were missionaries among the First Nations people of northern Canada and supported by our church, sent a request for young people to come help them for part of the summer. The commitment required us to cover our own travel expenses and work in a voluntary capacity while we were there.

On July 4, two friends and I left home on the long, two-day bus trip to northern Saskatchewan. We didn't know what to expect or exactly what we'd be doing. Audrey Goudsward (now Green) just had finished her first year of college, and Carlea Duerksen (now Williams) and I had completed grade eleven. We were young and ready for anything, and our church had rallied behind us in practical ways. For example, in addition to our personal luggage and musical instruments, my grandma and other women of the church had packed seven large cardboard boxes with clothing. It was our responsibility to deliver them to the Neudorfs for the people of their area. Each time we changed buses, we had to make sure that every box was accounted for and still intact.

Grandma was accustomed to preparing parcels for missionaries all over the world. Besides writing letters and mailing cassette tapes of our church services, she also prepared large packages of clothing for Ramabai Muktai Mission in India and containers for Tandala Hospital in Africa.

Every two years, three fifty-gallon metal drums destined for Tandala sat in her living room while she carefully packed them with bandages, baby layettes, and useful materials that she and other women from various churches had sewn. Having gathered the items over the two years, it took her a couple of weeks to pack the drums. She then arranged to have them trucked to the docks, where they were cleared by customs, loaded, and shipped to Africa. Our constant prayer was that the much-needed supplies would arrive safely.

Through her helping to deliver boxes of clothing to the people of the north and helping me learn to pack barrels for the children of Africa, Grandma taught me that there are people with greater needs than ours and that life is about more than just our little part of the globe. There's a big world out there, and God cares about each and every person in it.

When Audrey, Carlea, and I arrived at the northern-most point that the bus traveled, Van Neudorf drove us over the last leg of our journey to Dore Lake. The boxes were loaded into the back of Van's pick-up truck and delivered safely to the people.

Once we arrived at the village of Dore Lake, we discovered that there were no prepared lessons or materials for us to use to teach the children who would attend the meetings and camps. Instead, we had to develop our own lessons, create posters to promote the meetings, and prepare whatever teaching materials we wanted to use. It proved to be an invaluable learning experience, and I was grateful for the times I had spent assisting Grandma when she taught at our church's Daily Vacation Bible Schools.

After almost one month, Audrey and Carlea returned home. I, on the other hand, traveled for another month with a small team that drove throughout the province to teach Daily Vacation Bible Schools and work as counselors or support crew at Bible camps.

The daily journal I kept during that summer is filled with stories of the people I met and worked with, the adventures I experienced, and the lessons I learned. It was a great time of growth for me. One entry indicates that I was thinking about going to Bible school when I completed high school but I was concerned about my parents' response and whether or not that decision meant I'd have to give up my drums. It was a real struggle.

My time in Saskatchewan was in a positive, growing environment. The people whom I worked alongside mentored me in leadership and teaching, and I formed new friendships.

After two months of work and adventure, I left Saskatchewan and returned home to Grandma's. On my return, I discovered that a fellow I had met the week before I left for Saskatchewan wasn't as interested in me as I thought. After a very short conversation with him, I hung up the phone and said, "OK, God, I guess that wasn't meant to be. What's next?" I wasn't being flippant; I simply felt at peace and put the young sailor out of my mind. Little did I know what wonderful adventures were about to unfold in the coming year.

# CHAPTER 20

# Cross-Border Encounter

WITH A FEW days remaining before school was to start, I agreed to go to my parents' and look after my brothers while Mom and Dad went away. After six days, I returned to Grandma's to start my final year of high school.

That week, I received a letter from my close friend Pat Cogbill (now Massey), who was attending Multnomah School of the Bible. In her letter she wrote, "Oh, Ann, thank the Lord continually for where you are and how He has led you, and that He has given you a chance to learn right from the start, to draw all your comfort and strength from Him alone! Learn to do it, Ann. Be able to rejoice in Jesus whether those you love are there beside you or a million miles away. This I would share with you above anything else."

Today, as I reread the letter that I carefully placed in one of my scrapbooks more than forty years ago, I realize that those mentoring words of wisdom and encouragement still have worth.

At the beginning of grade twelve, I challenged the decision that had been made to transfer me from the university track into the general program when I was in grade ten. While in the general program, I learned skills like typing and bookkeeping, which proved to be useful in my adult years. But at the time, I believed the future held greater opportunities if I graduated on the university track.

Throughout grade eleven, I had talked often with the school counselor and confided in her about my desire to continue my education after high school. When I approached her with my plan to transfer back into the university entrance track, she encouraged me to do it but cautioned me about the hard work it would take to learn material I had missed and complete the graduation requirements all in one year. Nevertheless, I was determined and reminded her that I had taken a math course by correspondence in anticipation of making the change back to the university track.

The change meant that I had to catch up on the grade ten and eleven science, math, and French courses I had missed, while also keeping up with the grade twelve load required to graduate with my class. On my behalf, the counselor talked with the teachers involved and arranged for after-school and lunchtime sessions to help me get through it all.

It was a whirlwind year. I passed all of my final exams except French and history, which was a surprise because I loved history. Despite the shortfall in my grades, which meant that I did not officially complete grade twelve, I was permitted to attend my high school graduation and walk across the stage with my class. During that year, I also fulfilled my responsibilities as president of our church youth group, was an active member of the Surrey Schools' Concert Band, was awarded my high school's "Musician of the Year" award, and played percussion in the orchestra for the Surrey Musical Theater's Broadway production of *Brigadoon*.

One week after the theater's closing night of *Brigadoon*, I was talking with friends at church before the evening service began. It was March 17, 1968, and high school graduation was only two months away. When I looked toward the entrance of the church,

I was surprised to see the same fellow I had talked with on the phone the previous August.

I panicked. *I wonder if he'll recognize me. What if he talks to me?* My seventeen-year-old mind raced back to our short and formal phone conversation just months before, when it seemed that a relationship wasn't meant to be. But before I could think about what to say, he walked up the stairs to our little group and looked straight at me.

"Hi. I'm Jim. Do you remember me?"

*Do I remember him? How could I really forget?* When we met the previous year, I had thought there was a connection. But when I returned from Saskatchewan and he seemed distant, I put him out of my mind. Now that he stood in front of me, all the memories of that one evening at the skating rink, almost a year before, rushed back.

It had been an early summer evening the week before Audrey, Carlea, and I left for Saskatchewan. Our youth group was gathering at the church to head out for an evening of skating at a well-known roller rink across the Canada and United States border. Just as we were about to leave, Pastor Handy arrived and told a couple of us on the youth leadership team about a new young guy whom he had met that afternoon. He had invited him to join us for our event and wanted to be sure that we made him feel welcome.

When the fellow arrived on his motorcycle, I was rushing down the ramp outside the church to take care of something before we left. As I passed by him, I shot a quick, "Hi."

At the rink, my friend Audrey Green cheerfully introduced herself and some of us who were standing nearby. As we talked, we learned that his name was Jim and he recently had been honorably discharged from the Navy. When he later asked me to skate with him, I was surprised. *Why me?* He was so handsome, and I reasoned that there were girls in our group who were much better looking than I. Why hadn't he asked them?

Jim had a gentle yet edgy appeal to him that fascinated me. But he seemed out of bounds. He rode a motorcycle and wore a leather jacket—something done by people who ran with a gang or by the fellows that churchgoers wouldn't want their daughters or granddaughters to associate with.

Now here we were again—almost nine months since the first time we met. And he looked even better. His eyes were dark, deep-set, and kind. His hair was black and neatly combed. He was perfectly groomed and in clothes that made him look as handsome as he really was. He stood tall and straight, an obvious testament to his years of Navy training. He was every girl's dream of tall, dark, and handsome.

During the evening church service, Jim sat with me and my friends, but when everyone went downstairs for refreshments before the once-a-month music event known as *After Glow*, the two of us stayed seated in the sanctuary. We talked . . . and talked . . . and talked.

Jim explained that when we first met, he had just finished his stint in the Navy and was looking for someone to help sort out some of his questions about church and Christianity. He had driven by Johnston Heights Church and decided to go in. Pastor Handy talked and prayed with him and then invited him to join the youth group for a night of skating.

He went on to say that following our first meeting, he floundered in his new-found faith and felt he had failed as a Christian. He argued with God and tried to discover where he fit after finishing with the Navy. He also had been in a significant motorcycle accident and saw his cuts and bruises as a miracle that God was using to get his attention.

The accident was a turning point. He stopped fighting God, retired his bike, and recommitted his life to live for God. He said that since then he had wanted to come to church but felt too embarrassed about what had happened. When he finally made the decision to come that night, he was very concerned about what he'd say to me—if I was there.

From that night on, we spent as much time as possible together. But it didn't take me long to realize I had a dilemma.

Prior to Jim's coming back into my life, I had asked my lifelong friend Mel Anhorn to be my high school graduation date. At the time, he was living in Valdosta, Georgia, where he had gone into ministry after graduating from Prairie Bible Institute. He accepted my invitation and planned to arrive a couple of weeks prior to the graduation, which was set for May 24, 1968. My problem was that even though Mel and I liked each other and we each secretly had wondered if we might have a future together, I had grown very fond of Jim and loved being with him.

About two weeks before graduation, Mel arrived at his parents' home. On that Saturday, Jim and I went to the Christian bookstore that Grandma and I frequented when I was younger. As we walked past a store with graduation dresses displayed in the window, I knew I had to say something.

"You probably wonder why I haven't asked you to be my date for graduation, considering we've been doing a lot together," I began haltingly.

"Well, it had crossed my mind, but I thought you must have a reason," he replied.

"I really want you to be my date, but I can't ask you because I've already asked someone else," I continued.

As we walked together, I told him about Mel and that I had written and asked him a few months earlier to be my graduation date. I explained that he had accepted and I now felt obligated because he had traveled a long way and was my friend.

"I would like to go with you, but I understand. You don't have to explain. It's OK," Jim assured me.

That night and the next morning in church, my heart and head did battle. I wanted Jim to be my date, but I believed that I needed to be fair to Mel and honor my commitment.

Finally, that afternoon, I decided to walk to Mel's parents' house to talk it over with him. I barely had begun outlining my dilemma before he interrupted me.

"It's OK, Ann. You don't have to say anymore," he said with a warm smile. "When I saw you and Jim together, I knew there was something between you. It's so obvious. You belong together, and I think you should have Jim take you to your graduation."

That night at church, I introduced Mel to my friend May Bartram. May and I had been inseparable all through junior and senior high and were often at each other's homes.

Over the next two weeks Mel, May, Jim, and I went together to various events with friends. When graduation was only a couple of days away, May broke off with a fellow she had been dating for three years, and Mel became her date for graduation. The four of us had a wonderful time attending the graduation ceremonies together and joining in activities with other friends throughout that weekend.

The following year, Mel and May were married and returned to Valdosta, Georgia, to begin their life together.

One month after graduation, I was on the road again. This time, I would be gone for a much longer period.

# CHAPTER 21

# With Grandma's Blessing

S IX DAYS AFTER that Sunday night when Jim came back into my life, I was the maid of honor at my sister's wedding on March 23, 1968. Pat was sixteen, and I was seventeen. In the eleven years that had passed since our rainy-night ride to Grandma's in the big black car, we each had experienced journeys that took us down different paths. But we were sisters, and life would draw us closer in the coming years.

Three weeks after Pat's wedding, I was baptized at a Good Friday service. It was an important step in my public commitment as a Christian and marked the beginning of another phase of my life and walk with God. But it was a commitment that would be deeply tested in the years to come.

When high school graduation was over in May, I realized that going to university to study music wasn't going to happen, so I decided to pack my bags and spend another summer working with a ministry team in Saskatchewan. It was much like the summer before; only this time, I was one year older and had the experiences of the previous summer. As I traveled with a team, going from camp to camp and town to town, I was often given the responsibility of the young teen cabin or class, even though I wasn't much older than the teens themselves. Again, the summer adventure was a powerful training ground that fueled my desire to trust God more, helped me to see that I had choices, and prepared me for what lay ahead.

At the end of the summer of 1968, I went home to Grandma's with a longing to return to the small northern town of Big River, Saskatchewan. But I had no idea what I would do or how I would live. When I contacted the Carter family, whom I had met and worked with during the previous two summers, they said I could room and board with them for thirty dollars a month. Today, that sounds like a small amount, and even by the standards of that time, it was. But it was a fortune for me. I had no money and no job.

After I talked it over with Grandma and she received assurances that I would be safe with this family, I said my good-byes and boarded a bus for Saskatchewan. I had no idea what was ahead of me or how long I'd be away. I just knew that I needed to go.

As I look back, it amazes me how many times I set out on new adventures or took on new challenges—all with Grandma's blessing. Maybe she recognized her own independent and adventurous spirit in her granddaughter. Or maybe she knew that her experiences had made her stronger and built her faith. Now her granddaughter needed to learn similar lessons. Whatever the reason, I am grateful for the trust and freedom Grandma gave me in those years. They were years of monumental growth.

Once I was settled in at the Carters' home, which was about two miles outside of town, it was time to find a job. I walked up and down the main street numerous times. I passed the bank, two cafés, one hardware store, and one general store, with a few shops scattered among them. As I walked, I prayed, "Lord, I believe You want me here, but now I need to pay my way. I'm sure You have something worked out, so would You please let me know what it is? That place looks pretty good. What do You think? How about that one? No? OK, so where?"

After a couple days of walking around, I was drawn to one of the two cafés in town, even though I'd been told they probably weren't hiring because the family who owned it had twelve children of their own to do the work. On the day I decided to ask if they had work I could do, I walked back and forth on the opposite side of the street, watched who went in and out, and worked up the courage to cross the street and walk through the door.

When I finally stepped into the café, they were busy, so I waited.

After the preliminary questions about where I was from and where I was living, the woman asked, "Have you ever served customers? Do you know how to run a manual cash register?"

"Yes, ma'am. I learned at a drive-in theater a couple of summers ago."

"Well," she replied, "we were just saying this morning that we could use some help, especially during the day, now that most of the kids are back in school. We can't pay much, and we can't be sure how many hours you'll get."

I tried to be calm. "That's OK. Anything is a start. I need the work."

"Good. Your first job will be washing dishes. We don't have machines to do that. We do them all by hand, and they pile up fast. There's a strict way they have to be done. We never know when the health inspector will drop in to check that it's being done right."

I wasn't sure if she was trying to discourage me or wondering if my slight, hundred-pound frame was up to the job.

"I do all the cooking, but you'll have to help out with everything else. That means doing dishes, waiting on customers, cleaning shelves, and helping stock food deliveries. You'll also have to help wash the floor and clean up when you're here at closing time. Can you do all that?"

*Can I do that? You bet I can,* I thought. By her example, Grandma had shown me that no job was too small, and even when the work wasn't the most glamorous, it was important to do my best. She taught me that how I do my work reflects on who I am and makes a difference in what I will be trusted with in the future.

"Yes, I can do that," I replied. I was hired on the spot, at ninety-five cents an hour.

God stretched me during that one year in Big River. I experienced what it was like to live in a small-town conservative Christian home—where I was teased about being the city girl, even though I wasn't really from a big city. In the Carter home, TV was not yet allowed, discussions about appropriate dress and Christlike behavior were common, the radio was turned on only once a day to listen to the news, and there was always room for one more person around the table. Family devotions were strictly adhered to every morning, and each person took his or her designated morning to pray and read from the Bible and devotional book—no matter how old or how young he or she was. For this family, living one's faith was more than just words, and the rules were overshadowed by a deep love and respect for each other and a devoted willingness to help with whatever needed to be done.

During my time in Big River, I also became involved in the small Evangelical Free Church, where most of the attendees were related to the Carters. My job at the café gave me the opportunity to get to know the town's teenagers, whom I invited to youth activities at the church.

When I arrived in town, I felt like an outsider. When I moved away, I left people who had become my friends and some who were more like family. While I was there, I saw how one Christian family can affect the lives of a whole town. I adjusted to living with people whose taboos and opinions were a stark contrast to those I'd grown up with. I learned to listen to insights and opinions that were different from my own. And I came to realize that I had a rebellious spirit that needed to be reined in. Thankfully, the Carter family was very patient, and I came to love and respect them as if they were my own.

While there, I also served the church in whatever ways I could and got a lot of pleasure out of contributing and helping in ways that, to this day, are known only to me. I grew in my faith as I watched God mold my spirit and meet my needs. He supplied me with a family to live with, one that showed me a different side of family life. He broadened my world as I was introduced to missionaries, pastors, and Bible school students who were frequent guests at the Carter table. He provided me with a job in which I served business people and laborers during the day and teenagers at night. It was a job that earned me enough money to meet my commitments and needs while in Big River and allowed me to take the next step of my life journey.

After almost a year in northern Saskatchewan, I traveled home to British Columbia to visit friends and family and pull together what I needed for the coming year at Bible school, where I would live in a dorm. I was grateful for the bedding, school materials, and winter clothes I was able to purchase with the money I'd earned at the café. And I was thankful for Grandma, who used her skills as a seamstress to make skirts and dresses that met the school's mid-knee skirt length regulation.

I was off on another adventure, but not before Jim placed a promise ring on my finger. The school rules stipulated that once a person was accepted as a student, he or she could not become engaged or married without the school's permission. However, there was nothing that said anything about a promise ring. For Jim, the stunning blue star sapphire set on a gold band was his way of making himself feel like he had at least "laid his claim."

Ann (12) dressed in Fireman's Band uniform, with her first drum, 1962

Surrey Schools Concert Band. Ann (16) stands top left, 1966

Able Seaman Jim Griffiths (18), 1965

Jim (20) on leave with his motorcycle, 1967

Jim (22) and Ann (19),
May 1969

Ann at Bible
school, 1969

# CHAPTER 22

# The Missing Link

AT THE END of one month at Grandma's, I was off to the southern part of Saskatchewan, to what is now known as Millar College of the Bible. I have fond memories of life at Millar and believe that I would have missed out on so much if I never had attended. Sometimes I wonder what direction my life would have taken if I had stayed for the full three-year program.

During the one year I attended, I was exposed to many new people and things, including dorm life and "gratis," which was the term used to describe the chores given to each student to minimize his or her tuition costs. My assignment was the ironing crew, which worked in a long narrow basement room.

When you entered the room, you were immediately greeted by a deep row of ironing boards that were lined up one behind the other. To the right, there was barely enough space to walk past the row of boards to the far wall, where there was a small window high above our reach. Every Thursday, the ironing crew came together to press, among other things, an endless stack of white cotton shirts that were dropped off by the male students for washing and ironing at the campus laundry. When I saw students going off to the kitchen before meals to set the tables or staying behind after meals as part of the dish washing or pot scrubbing crews, I was grateful I could get all my gratis done in one afternoon each week so I could spend more time doing other things.

In classes, I received solid theological and biblical teaching, as well as practical lessons in areas like etiquette, grammar, missions, and public speaking. The year also introduced me to people from different parts of the world and enabled me to explore a variety of ways one could make a difference. When a unique opportunity came up to pioneer a drop-in coffee house ministry with three other students, I jumped at it. We were concerned about the teens in the tiny town that bordered the edge of our small campus and wanted a place where they could come to talk, play games, and listen to music. After presenting our plan to the powers that be, we received permission to use an empty, abandoned house in town. We named it *The Missing Link* and enlisted other students to help us work with the teens and share the gospel with them.

Millar is also where I met Mrs. Folkford, who was the dean of women I wrote about in the book *A Mentor's Fingerprint*. She "was a tall, gray-haired woman with a reputation for being a strict, no-nonsense individual. But, for me, Mrs. Folkford always had a twinkle in her eye—even when she caught me pushing the rule book boundaries or instigating dorm pranks."

At a time when the mini skirt was the style but Bible school rules demanded that our skirts and dresses be no shorter than mid-knee, my rebel side showed its face. When I didn't think teachers or staff were looking, I rolled my skirt up at the waist so that my skirt length came to two or three inches above my knee. When I saw someone coming, like our dean of women, I quickly rolled it back down. I also sometimes let the ring Jim gave me, which I wore on my left ring finger, twist around to look like a wedding band. I wanted to see if Mrs. Folkford would react to my mischievous nature, which was alive and well. But she never did.

When she administered discipline, her example "taught me that a calm response can often be more effective than a long lecture and stern look, although they too may have their place. She also demonstrated that what's in the heart of a person affects how she acts—even in the midst of foolishness. And that fun is fun, but one must be accountable and take responsibility for the outcome of the fun." What a wonderful affirmation of the lessons I had learned from my grandma as I was growing up!

From the fall of 1968 through the spring of 1970, when I was in Big River and Bible school, Grandma and Jim both sent me weekly letters by mail. Grandma also periodically sent care packages of cookies and treats that I shared with my roommate.

I treasured every letter I received from them and still have all the ones Jim sent. In one of Grandma's letters that I kept, which she sent shortly after Jim returned from spending the Christmas of 1968 with me in Big River, she wrote, "Jim told me that he was going steady with you. I said that I had figured that out. I expect you remember what I said once—that I hoped when the time came you would marry a good Christian boy."

One of the benefits of my time away was the bond that formed between my grandma and Jim. During that time, Grandma went from being unimpressed and almost standoffish with the former Navy boy who rode a motorcycle, wore a leather jacket and blue jeans, and showed interest in her granddaughter, to loving him as a grandson and being willing to do anything for him.

At the end of my year of Bible school, I decided to spend the summer at home with Grandma and work as the volunteer assistant to Len Roberts, who had been hired as the first youth pastor of my home church, Johnston Heights Evangelical Free Church. That experience launched a friendship with Len and his wife, Jean, that grew through many years of ministering together. In the early years of that lifelong friendship, Len mentored Jim and me in how to think and plan strategically, practically apply the gospel to life and ministry, and organize teams to focus them toward a vision.

During that summer of 1970, I immersed myself in whatever needed to be done for the church's youth ministry. Working with Len, I edited and typed letters, brainstormed ideas, painted rooms, and knocked down walls in what would become a thriving coffee house and youth center. Churches were changing how they reached out to young people, and I loved being on the cutting edge of something new. I believed I was making a difference and contributing to something important. As a result, I decided to continue volunteering at the church, find a paying job, and not return to Bible school.

Early in the fall, we opened a coffee house in the older part of the church and adopted the name *The Missing Link*—the same name as the coffee house I was involved in at Bible school. Every weekend we saw upwards of three hundred teens come through the doors, while high school students and young adults from the church served as volunteers on teams ranging from security, games, and kitchen crews to counseling, clean-up, and music teams.

Together, Jim and I worked with Len and the people he brought together to reach out to teens who came from a variety of backgrounds, from church-savvy to street-smart kids. While Jim was Len's right-hand man and oversaw the security and counseling teams that interacted with the teens, I continued assisting Len and became the drummer in the band. Soon the band was also playing at other churches and outdoor youth events in the area.

During this time, Jim worked on his bricklaying apprenticeship, and I studied criminology at the local community college, where I also worked part time in the library.

One Saturday night, after a very full and active evening at *The Missing Link,* Jim and I decided not to unwind with the rest of the team at a 24-hour café. Instead, we chose to go for a drive and ended up at the popular Burnaby Mountain view point.

As the clock ticked us into Thanksgiving Sunday and we were about to drive back down the mountain, Jim got a cramp in his foot. After he reached down to massage it, he came back up with something in his hand.

Turning to face me, he opened a small box and asked, "Will you marry me?"

## PERSONAL REFLECTION

1. Who influenced the choices you made as a teenager or young adult? How did he or she help you?

2. Has there been a family outside of your own that had a deep and lasting impact on your life? What did you learn from them? What difference did they make in your life?

3. What roles/responsibilities did you have in your teen years? What specific life experiences taught you about boundaries and responsibility?

4. As your grandchildren go from one stage of life to another they will make decisions that could affect the direction of their life. As their grandparent, how can you best help them in that process?

5. Recall a humorous story from your high school or post-secondary school years and share it with your grandchildren.

6. For your grandchildren, write a short story of how you and your spouse met.

# CHAPTER 23

# Modern-Day Miracles

LATER LEARNED THAT because Jim had hidden the box under the driver's seat of the car, he needed to find a way to reach for it discreetly. But because he reasoned that he didn't want to lie to me about a cramp in his foot, he deliberately made himself get one.

How could I say "no" to a man who demonstrated that he never would lie to me?

When I returned home in the early hours of the morning, I knew that Grandma would be awake. She rarely stayed up, but no matter what time I returned home, she always was awake in bed and waiting to hear me come through the front door.

I was excited to surprise her and show her the beautiful diamond set between four smaller diamonds. But as I stepped into her room, Grandma's face beamed with a knowing smile.

In later years, Grandma and I often teased each other about who had the best man.

"I was married to the two best men in the world," Grandma chided.

"That's impossible because I have the best man in the world," I replied.

Then we chuckled and gave each other a one-armed, knowing hug.

When Jim and I got engaged, it was still considered courteous for a young man to talk with a girl's parents before he asked her to marry him. But instead of talking with my parents, Jim went to my grandma. She had made a massive difference in my life, and I now saw that she had influenced Jim so much that he chose to talk with her about marrying me.

Grandma continued to make a difference in our lives when we became husband and wife and, later, parents. She also would leave an indelible mark on the lives of our future children.

While others helped us with specific needs for our upcoming wedding, Grandma sewed, baked, and wrapped. She also offered suggestions for our ceremony and reception. When I couldn't find a wedding dress I liked or could afford, she pieced parts of three different patterns together to make a new design and sewed a "test" dress out of scrap materials of different weights and colors. Once I had modeled the dress of many colors for our private photo shoot and Grandma was satisfied that the new design worked, we purchased all the right accessories and fabric, and Grandma created a beautiful wedding dress masterpiece—complete with a full-length train and veil.

A couple of months prior to the big day, Grandma made our wedding cake so that the flavors had time to permeate the three-layered, traditional English, dark fruit cake before it was iced. She also helped fold programs and cut and wrap individual pieces of cake for our guests to take home.

On June 19, 1971, Jim and I were married in front of two hundred friends and family. I was twenty-one, attending Douglas College, and working part-time at the college library. Jim was twenty-four, taking night courses to finish high school, and working as an apprentice journeyman bricklayer.

Our wedding party consisted of four attendants for each of us and included Jim's brother and sister and my sister. My brother Ian and one of Jim's cousins were candle lighters; my eldest brother, Bert, was one of the ushers; my youngest brother, David, was ring bearer; and my sister's two-year-old daughter, Susette, was our flower girl.

The ceremony was scheduled to take place at 6:30 P.M., but one photo of my dad and me coming down the aisle shows 7:00 P.M. on the clock at the back of the church. Everything had been planned perfectly, but I had neglected to account for my dad, who liked to start drinking early in the day, especially on a weekend. When he arrived at Grandma's to take me to the church, he was late—and drunk. My memory of him walking me down the aisle is that I wasn't sure who was holding up whom. When I went from my dad's arm to Jim's, I felt like I was stepping from one world into another.

At that moment, the flood gates sprang a leak. I started to cry and struggled to control the tears throughout the ceremony. It was the first time I'd given myself permission to cry since the vow I'd taken ten years earlier, when I was eleven years old.

Four weeks after our wedding, I woke up in the morning to a husband who had been up most of the night and now believed that God wanted him to go to university to get his degree in psychology. During the next month, we witnessed miracle after miracle as we trusted God for our future.

First, Jim was accepted to Trinity Junior College (now known as Trinity Western University). This was a miracle because he had not graduated from high school and his official records had been destroyed in a fire three years earlier. On July 25, he submitted his application with letters of recommendation. Three days later, on July 28, we received word that he had been conditionally accepted—just in time for us to give month-end notice on our apartment, even though we didn't have a place to move to. Jim would be on academic probation for the first semester, but he was in.

Our second and third miracles were getting an apartment in the married students' facilities on campus and a job for me. We needed to live and work on campus in order to keep costs to a minimum, but there were no apartments or suitable jobs available on campus. On July 29, we received a call to tell us that a couple had become ill and would not be able to attend school, making their apartment available for us. On the same call, I was offered the only full-time position in the library other than the librarian's.

Over the next month, we tied up loose ends and prayed for the funds we needed. Our first financial miracle came after we were told that on registration day, September 3, we needed $120 to pay the mandatory one-third down payment on Jim's first semester tuition. We didn't have $120, but on September 3, I was paid for two weeks' work. From that $134 check, we paid Jim's down payment and bought $14 worth of groceries.

Using our VW bug and Jim's parents' car, we moved our few belongings to our new one-bedroom apartment and settled in for two years of campus life. With Jim's periodic bricklaying projects, my campus job, student grants and scholarships, gifts of food from friends and family, and anonymous gifts to Jim's student account, our every need was met.

Due to a shortage of discretionary funds, we only drove our car on weekends. On Saturdays, we did errands, visited Jim's family, helped Grandma with odd jobs around her house, volunteered at the coffee house in the evening, and stayed overnight at Grandma's. On Sundays, we went to church and then had lunch with Grandma before heading back to campus.

Periodically, Jim's mom discretely squeezed ten or fifteen dollars into his hand as we said "good-bye" at the door after a visit. And almost every weekend, Grandma sent us home with a large brown paper bag of groceries she'd purchased for us. At the bottom of the bag of necessities, we always found a special treat—usually a package of popcorn or Licorice Allsort candies.

I can't help but be reminded of how careful Grandma was with her money and the sacrifices she must have made to provide those groceries for us. Even though we lived on a limited income, with half my salary going to rent, she lived on a senior's pension. Yet she gave out of what she had, and she gave without hesitation. To this day, we are grateful for her gifts and the gifts and support of friends and family who helped us during those early days of our marriage.

Grandma taught me a lot about money by how she managed her finances and by the nuggets of financial wisdom she instilled in me as I was growing up. I remember her saying things like, "If you don't have the money to pay for something, don't buy it." She was opposed to being in debt and always cautioned me about credit cards. In her later years, she was obliged to get a credit card, but true to her convictions, she told me, "Any time I want to write a check, I have to show ID. But I don't have a driver's license, so I got this for identification."

When she bought something with the card, she'd say, "I use it from time to time to keep it active, but I never use it unless I know I have the money to pay it off before it's due. That way I don't have to pay interest."

While I'm confident that credit companies never made money off Grandma, I wish that in my young adult years I had paid more attention to her advice. Thankfully, it rings loud and clear for me today, and I am grateful for her practical wisdom and guidance.

# CHAPTER 24

# A Lesson in Grace

ONCE I WAS married, Grandma's involvement in my life changed. Yet, as I went through her diaries during the writing of this book, I was reminded of how much she was there for us and continued to play a major role in our lives.

When Jim finished at Trinity in the spring of 1973 with high honors, he was accepted to the University of Victoria, where he planned to complete his degree. While we made arrangements to move to Victoria, our friend Len Roberts told us he was resigning from the church's youth pastor position to start a ministry to underprivileged youth and juvenile offenders in our city. He wanted Jim to take a year out of his education to help get the ministry off the ground.

After talking and praying about it, we accepted the challenge. Stepping into this new venture, we had no idea that our first year with One Way Adventure Foundation would turn into four years and two children before Jim could return to his formal education.

During those four years, Jim worked closely with Len, and within the first weeks, we became acutely aware of the many teens who had no place to call home. As part of our work with these young people, Len and Jean and Jim and I became government-approved foster parents.

Before the summer was over, God had changed our direction from continuing university and living in a small apartment for the two of us to working in a ministry to young offenders and underprivileged youth and living in a three-level townhouse with a male boarder and two teenage boys. It was official now—we had become foster parents to teenagers before we even had children of our own.

The boys who came into our lives during that time ranged in age from fourteen to sixteen and were known to the police. But they needed a home. They were boys who had been rejected by their families and experienced every government program available to them, including juvenile detention. To survive, they had learned from others who also were known to the police, and they had grown suspicious of anyone who tried to help them and expected nothing in return.

The boys' backgrounds represented an array of offenses and challenges. They were con artists, break-and-enter felons, and drug addicts. On one occasion, we had a boy living with us who was involved in the occult and another whom the police suspected of attempting to kill his parents. Despite their situations, they were all boys who needed a safe family environment that provided discipline and boundaries with love.

Two months into the fall of 1973, I underwent emergency surgery, and once again, Grandma stepped in. While I was in the hospital, and later as I recovered, Grandma came to our home every day to cook and clean for our house full of testosterone. This act of service should come as no surprise, as her diaries are full of notes about her helping friends and family during periods of illness. Yet I am grateful and reminded again of her sacrificial spirit—especially considering the crew she had to care for.

By the spring of 1974, One Way had about forty teens involved in day programs, supported twelve to fifteen staff, and provided government-approved foster care through select staff couples. In addition to our being asked to accept more kids into our programs, we were receiving requests from other communities that wanted help with their troubled teens. We needed more space and more staff.

As the demand grew, Len heard of a piece of property that was for sale in the small town of Hedley, British Columbia, and was situated two hundred miles from where we were located in Surrey, a suburb of Vancouver. From the start of the ministry, his dream had been to provide an environment where teens could learn and grow without the negative influences that most of them were accustomed to in the city. This out-of-the-city location would allow for that dream to become a reality and provide the opportunity to help teens in other areas of the province.

Through a series of miracles, funds came available to put a down payment on the property. During March of 1974, Jim and I, who were now expecting our first child, moved to the grounds to oversee the work while Len and Jean remained "at the coast" to continue operating the base ministry.

The property was located in the picturesque Similkameen Valley, with mountains on both sides. It had acres of land and two primary buildings that were built in the post gold-rush era of the early 1900s. The colonial style buildings, with wrap-around porches, large stone fireplaces, and multiple rooms, had been used as offices and housing for the mine owners.

When the rush for gold was over, the property and buildings had passed through different hands, until they finally were left abandoned and used by transients. The buildings were in desperate need of repair. The restoration and renovation was no small undertaking, but it became a starting point for the practical ways we built relationships with the teens who came to work and learn under our care.

Jim and I initially lived in a room of one of the buildings, while another couple with their young son lived in another room.

Together we cooked our meals on a camp stove until the facilities were operational. A couple months later, Jim and I purchased a mobile home and lived in it with our friends and co-workers, Paul and Marie Weston and their toddler son. After the birth of our first child, and a few months of four adults and two children sharing a twelve-by-sixty-eight-foot space, we decided to move the mobile home onto the One Way property to be more available for the growing needs of the organization. Paul and Marie found alternate housing while we continued on as foster parents to one boy who lived with us. We also provided meals for junior staff who lived elsewhere on the campus.

During the three and a half years we were in the little town of Hedley, we made numerous trips back to "the coast," where we stayed with Grandma. On many occasions, due to the demands of the work, we drove to Surrey one day and returned to Hedley the next.

After one weekend trip, we learned that the foster son we had taken with us had stolen some old coins from Grandma's dresser and sold them. For Grandma, the coins were mementos of her early years in England, and while they had some monetary value, it was the sentiment behind them that was more important to her. I could tell that Grandma was hurt and upset over the loss. But I was angry. I couldn't understand how, after we had welcomed the boy into our home, loved him, and shared my grandma with him, he could betray our trust and steal from her. What had she ever done to him? I reasoned that it would have been better if he had stolen from me rather than from my grandma.

While the coins never were found, Grandma chose to exercise grace and refused to call the police or lay charges against the boy. And though none of us spoke of the matter again, Jim and I chose never to take another foster boy to my grandma's home.

# CHAPTER 25

# Hope in Life's Desert

ON SEPTEMBER 22, 1974, we were blessed with our own baby girl. But there was a problem.

Within hours of Sarah's birth, the doctor told us that she had congenital hip—an abnormal formation of the hip joint that makes the sufferer walk with a pronounced limp and causes other long-term difficulties. The condition is often not detected until the child begins to walk, but the attending nurse had noticed something out of the ordinary when she examined our baby in the delivery room and had alerted our doctor. Sarah immediately had multiple diapers put on her little body to keep her legs apart and her hips in place. I had never heard of congenital hip and had no idea what it meant for our daughter.

In those days, babies didn't stay in the hospital room with their mothers. At specific times, they were brought to us for feeding, and during visiting hours, they were displayed in their bassinets behind the nursery window so visitors could see them. I remember watching her through the window and hearing other parents and their friends comment about the baby who looked "like a frog in all those diapers." I wanted to hold her close and tell her how beautiful she was and how much God and her daddy and I loved her.

At two days old, Sarah was put into a full body cast that went from under her arms to just above her knees and kept her legs spread apart. I quickly learned to nurse and hold her awkward shape so that neither of us felt uncomfortable. After an extended time in the hospital, Sarah and I stayed with Grandma until the cast could be removed. Meanwhile, Jim looked after the demands of his work and our busy household in Hedley and drove the two hundred miles each way from Hedley to Surrey to spend weekends with us.

While Sarah had her cast on, the doctor said that no one was permitted to hold her except Jim and me and Grandma, who helped care for her. As Sarah could not be diapered, I was grateful for Grandma's help with the extra cleaning and washing and for her "stiff upper lip" words of encouragement. Her attitude that "this is the way it is for now, and we're going to make the best of it because our baby needs love and care no matter how we feel" was the same attitude she had modeled throughout so much of my life. It was now my turn to put that same discipline into action for my own little family.

It seemed like several weeks before the doctor told us the cast could come off, but in reality it was only seventeen days. When the day came, we were told that because Sarah was a baby, the cast could not be taken off in the usual way—with a loud saw at the hospital. Instead, we had to remove it manually by ourselves—at home.

The process took the better part of a day. Between naps and feeding times, we immersed Sarah in warm water to soften the layers of gauze and plaster that formed the cast. While I cradled Sarah on my left arm, which was submerged in the plastic baby bathtub on the kitchen table, I kept her entertained with singing and toys. Meanwhile, Grandma carefully snipped edges of the softened layers with scissors and tore them away, piece by piece, with her fingernails. We tried to make it as easy as possible for Sarah so the ordeal would not traumatize her. We must have succeeded, because at one point, she was so relaxed that she fell asleep in the warm water while we both worked on cutting and peeling the layers of gauze and plaster. I never could have done it without Grandma.

Once the body cast was removed and we settled back into a relatively normal life in Hedley, Sarah became the reason for a decision that changed the mix of people living in our bustling mobile home.

Over the years, Grandma had taught me to pay attention to "the still, small voice inside of me." One day, when Sarah was less than a year old, that "still, small voice" screamed out loud and clear.

Sarah was lying on her blanket on the floor and reaching for an overhead toy while one of our foster boys sat on the floor, talking and playing with her. As I watched them play, a strong but calm feeling came over me, and I knew we needed to stop being foster parents. Whether or not anything bad could have happened, I can only imagine (if I let myself). What I do believe is that God impressed on me the importance of protecting our little girl. Though I haven't always listened to that "still, small voice" the way I should have over the years, I am happy that I did then. And I have never regretted the decision we made.

Sarah Ann was God's special gift to us. When she took her first steps at seventeen months of age, she began a journey of more casts, metal leg braces, and brown lace-up Oxford leather boots that she had to wear twenty-three hours a day. A portion of the upper part of the boot was cut away so her toes could peek through and air could circulate. She also wore the boots on opposite feet to help correct the direction her feet naturally wanted to turn. By the time she entered school, she was like any other child who enjoyed running and playing.

Seventeen months after Sarah's birth, our son, James Samuel, was born on March 9, 1976. After careful examination, we were assured that he had not been born with the same physical issues as Sarah. But over the next few days, he presented us with a different challenge and eventually was diagnosed with severe colic.

Though he was fed and clean, James cried almost every moment—unless he was asleep, which was seldom. Nothing seemed to calm him. When I nursed him, he fussed constantly. When I paced the floor with him, he fussed and cried. When I laid him down, he fussed and cried and screamed. I tried everything from old-fashioned remedies to any new ideas friends offered me. But nothing worked. When Jim came in the door at the end of the day, I was at my wit's end. I pushed James into Jim's arms and said things like, "Here's your son. You do something with him." James cried all the time. Sleep was almost impossible for all of us.

After two months, the doctor said that the only thing he could do for us was to prescribe a sedative for our baby or for me. I refused on both counts. I wasn't about to sedate our son, and because I was nursing him, I didn't want to take something I thought could harm him. I also reasoned that colic was only supposed to last the first three months of a baby's life, and we already had made it through two of those months. I was sure we could make it through one more. But I was about to find out that God had blessed us with a son that was his own person and wouldn't always do the expected.

As it turned out, James and the rest of us endured his colicky condition for four and a half months. When that ordeal was over, he started letting us know about each and every tooth he cut.

A week after I declined the doctor's offer to prescribe a sedative, Jim's wonderful mother turned fifty years old. One week later, we received a phone call that she had died suddenly at home, cradled in Dad's arms. It was a hard blow for all of us.

In the midst of James's colicky stage, the loss of Jim's mom, and our growing responsibilities, I felt pushed to the limit and began to ask, "Where are You, God?" I came to understand, in a small way, how some mothers could unintentionally be pushed to the edge of hurting their child. Thankfully, I never went that far, but I certainly felt like I came close as I became frustrated with not being able to console our little son. In all of it, God taught me two valuable lessons—one through a book and the other through my grandma.

One day, in desperation, I sat cross-legged on the floor in front of our bookcase that lined the wall of our mobile home living room. I needed to read something, but what? I loved books, but it seemed like a lifetime had passed since I'd had time or energy to read anything. Scanning the shelves, my eyes fell on one hardcover volume that I hadn't read before.

Over the next few days, I devoured the book *Something More* by Catherine Marshall. It changed my perspective on my life, and I learned that because I am a child of God, He holds me in His arms and knows all about what is going on in my life. Because I am wrapped in His love, nothing can touch me unless He first steps aside and allows it. I realized that if God allows something to come into my life, it is for my growth and His purpose—and He will never leave me while I am in the middle of it. I also learned the need to acknowledge God's presence and thank and praise Him for what is happening in my life. Ultimately, He is in control.

I remember saying, "OK, Lord, I can acknowledge Your presence, and I can thank You for what's going on because I know You must have a reason for it all. But, praise You for it? I'm not so sure about that. I know I need to do it, but it's not easy."

Standing at my kitchen sink, I looked out the window at the sandy soil and rocks that surrounded our mobile home. Tufts of grass poked up between the rocks and added texture to the barren soil. I didn't have time to plant and nurture flower boxes to add bright colors of red and yellow and orange to the landscape, but I loved flowers.

As I looked over the scene in front of me, I thought about what God was teaching me. I wondered how I could praise Him in my situation—when I didn't feel like it. Then He showed me that it was OK to start with the little things in life.

With my hands in dishwater, I noticed a single wildflower just outside my kitchen window. It stood all alone among the rocks, the sand, and the tufts of grass, but it was gently waving back and forth to the soft rhythms of the spring breeze.

That day, God used the principles from Catherine Marshall's book and a lone flower outside my kitchen window to teach me a valuable lesson during a difficult time. In time, I moved from praising Him for the little flower outside my window to praising Him for what He had allowed in my life and what He would do with it.

The other valuable lesson I learned during this time came through Grandma. But not in the way one might think.

Grandma always had been there for me, but this time, she didn't run to my side and offer practical help and pearls of wisdom. Instead, when I asked her to come to Hedley to help me, she did something totally out of character and told me she couldn't come.

I felt let down and overwhelmed. I was cooking for three junior staff, who ate their meals in our home; Jim was on call 24/7; and I had a colicky new baby and a toddler who had only taken her first steps the week before James was born, even though she was talking and putting words into sentences. I needed help—desperately. But when I asked Grandma to come and help me get through the first weeks after James's birth, she said she couldn't come. I felt alone and couldn't understand what could be more important. Yet even in that situation, Grandma left her fingerprint on my life and taught me something I didn't comprehend until years later, when

I too became a grandma. I never fully learned her reasons for not coming, but I came to understand that grandmas can't always be where grandmas would like to be or do what they'd like to do for those they love.

Despite the challenges, we all made it through that first year of James's life. He became an energetic boy, whose antics often drove us to the hospital for bones to be mended or cuts to be stitched. Grandma often used to say, "That boy doesn't know how to walk. He only knows how to run." But despite his active body and early months of constant crying, James had a tender heart that shone through in his love for animals and their love for him. It was not unusual for us to find him and a friendly dog cuddled up together under a tree on a hot summer day.

# CHAPTER 26

# An Unpredictable Maze

OVER THE NEXT four years, we all learned to maneuver a maze of transition and change. When I look at Grandma's diaries from 1977 through 1980, I am in awe of how she actively walked through that maze with us. For me, those years were a blur of children and doctors, ministry and work, moving and school. But while certain highlights are cemented in my memory, other events are lost in the fog. Thankfully, Grandma's detailed accounts and my journals help me to bring the blurry events and situations into focus.

In April of 1977, Jim's best friend, Paul Weston, died of cancer at the age of twenty-eight. Paul's funeral was to be held almost seven hundred miles away, in the neighboring province of Alberta. He and Marie had moved there from Hedley with their young son to be near Paul's parents during his illness. The challenge for Jim was that he had been asked to serve as one of the pallbearers and wanted to be there for our friends, but the funeral was scheduled for the same day that Jim was to be best man at his dad's wedding in Vancouver.

Our solution was for Jim to fly seven hundred miles east to Alberta to be with our friends and serve as a pallbearer while I and our two babies drove two hundred miles southwest to attend Jim's dad's wedding ceremony in Surrey. Thankfully, Grandma took care of our two children on the wedding day.

Arrangements were made for Jim's uncle to step in as best man for the ceremony and for Jim to fly to the Vancouver International Airport as soon as the funeral was over in Alberta. Jim's brother met him at the airport and drove him to their dad's wedding reception, where we all finished off the evening together. It was a roller-coaster day of emotions.

That fall, Jim began full-time studies at Simon Fraser University—four years after leaving school to help our friends Len and Jean Roberts start the ministry of One Way, which we still were involved in. For the remaining months of 1977, we traveled the two hundred miles back and forth between Hedley and Surrey. On weekdays, we stayed in Surrey with Grandma while Jim studied and attended classes. On most weekends and during vacation times, we worked in Hedley with the various groups that went to the One Way facilities for camps and retreats. And we spent a lot of time at the hospital with our children.

In July, our two-year-old daughter, Sarah, got into a newly purchased "child-proof" bottle of children's aspirin that Jim had brought home from the store. While we were in another room with Grandma, Sarah ate all twenty-four tablets, which necessitated a rush trip to the hospital to have her stomach pumped.

In September, our active eighteen-month-old son, James, jumped off Grandma's couch and broke his elbow. The next day, wearing a cast and sling, he seemed determined to do the same thing all over again—first from the couch and then from the outside porch. I suppose it should be no surprise that we have photos of him later competing in high-jump at school track and field meets.

To round out the year, on December 19, Sarah had casts put on both her legs as part of the treatments to correct her feet. This was left over from the congenital hip condition she was born with.

The next year, from January through early May of 1978, Grandma's home was our home, where we lived most of the time. While Jim continued his studies at the university during the week and traveled to Hedley to work with camps on weekends, I worked on-call at the Surrey Public Library. It was five months of juggling schedules so Grandma, Jim, or I could be with the children. Thankfully, we were all flexible—not only with schedules but also in our attitudes toward the situation.

Looking back, I can't help but think that it must have been difficult for my almost eighty-year-old grandma to deal with extra people coming and going and with the unpredictable schedules we kept. It's good that we all knew there was a light at the end of the tunnel and that "this too shall pass." But I wonder if Grandma had flashbacks to when I was young and my parents and five children were living with her.

During the early months of 1978, we sold our Hedley mobile home to One Way for use as staff housing and put our furniture and belongings into storage in Surrey—a sure sign that we did not intend to return to Hedley. However, in May, at the end of Jim's winter/spring semester, we agreed to move back to Hedley to work for the summer season. Our responsibilities were to focus on the operations of the camp and retreat groups and to start a bed and breakfast in the main building, which was known as The Colonial Lodge.

Since other staff members were living in our old mobile home, our family of four was given one room in The Colonial Lodge. The twelve-by-twelve room with an attached bathroom opened into the lobby of the lodge and put us right in the middle of all the activities, which included groups coming and going for camps and retreats, bed and breakfast guests, the central office, and the resident teens and staff. There was a constant flow of people.

From May through the summer, we lived in the Lodge, and though our children and the work demands kept us very busy, we enjoyed the variety of people who came through the doors. We also were grateful for other One Way staff members who worked in the ministry with us and became our friends.

Due to our unique living situation, our children learned to communicate with people of all ages and from different walks of life. They learned to be flexible, to welcome people into our home, and to respect the privacy of others. They also learned that they may have had the run of the massive Colonial Lodge when people weren't there, but when guests arrived, there were restrictions and strict boundaries.

At the end of the summer, Jim and I decided that it was best for the children and me to stay at The Colonial Lodge and not go back and forth between Hedley and Surrey. James just had undergone surgery on the arm he had broken the year before, and Sarah was still in special shoes and leg braces.

While the children and I remained and worked in the Lodge, Jim traveled to the coast. On Sundays, he took a bus to Surrey and stayed at my grandma's while attending classes during the week. On Friday afternoons, rather than driving our car through the mountains in winter, he boarded a bus and traveled back to our little family. Together, we worked through the weekend with groups that were there for retreats.

After four months of this routine, we concluded that the separation was harder on all of us than we had anticipated. So on Tuesday, January 2, 1979, we moved back to the coast permanently and arrived at Grandma's, where we were welcomed with open arms.

Within the next five days, I began a part-time job at the Trinity Western library; we moved to a two-bedroom apartment in the men's dorm at Trinity where, in lieu of rent, we served as dorm supervisors; and Jim started his final winter/spring and summer semesters at nearby Simon Fraser University while working with One Way in the Surrey office.

But life was about to take on new twists and turns for all of us—including Grandma.

Ann and Grandma, 1973

Grandma with great-grandchildren James (1) and Sarah (2), July 1977

Grandma and Ann, 1980

Ann and Jim with Youth for
Christ on the Great Wall of
China, August 1984

Flora Macalister, a friend who provided new clothes for us children when we were young, Grandma, and Ann, November 1984

Our family: James (11), Sarah (12), Ann, and Jim, 1987

Ann with her grandchildren Anthony (6), Calista (4), Victoria (8), May 2005

Siblings (l to r): Bert, Keith, Trevor, Pat, Ian, Ann, David, 2008.
Not shown: Eric who passed away in 1993 at 29 years old

Ann and her granddaughter, Victoria (12), 2009

Our family: Victoria (13), Sherman, Sarah, Anthony (11), Jim, Ann, Calista (9), James, August 2010

# CHAPTER 27

# Restless but Grounded

N THE EIGHT months that our little family lived in the men's dorm at Trinity Western, I began having troubling thoughts about my life. From the time I was a young girl, I had dreamed of making a mark on the world, but at twenty-nine years of age, I felt like I hadn't done anything significant. I got married and abandoned my education to help my husband through university. I worked in many facets of full-time ministry and had a number of foster boys in our home. I had two children who were now four and five years old. Life was full. But I felt like I wasn't doing anything to make a difference in the world. Time was running out—or so I thought.

Sometimes I'd tell myself that maybe the mark I would leave would be the influence I had on my children and what they eventually would do with their lives. But I struggled. I loved my marriage, my children, and my home. But I felt like there was something more for me.

Whether Grandma sensed the restlessness in me or I talked with her about it, I don't remember. But I do remember that during this time, it was Grandma who pointed me in the direction that would change the course of my life.

After inviting me to some women's events, she encouraged me to become involved with the ministry the church had with women. In those days, it was called the Women's Missionary Society. In the future, it would take on a whole new look and become known as Women's Ministries. I am blessed to have been on the leading edge of the changes that built on the strong foundation laid by pioneer women like my grandma.

That early involvement, along with the mentoring and modeling I received from Grandma and other women, led me to many opportunities where I served in leadership roles and pioneered new ventures. On one occasion, when I was being sworn in as president for the Lower Pacific District of Women's Ministries, my grandma was asked to say a few words about me. The other day, I found the notes she used for her short speech, and I was reminded again of the role she played in my life. The last line of her speech read, "I think Ann was born to be a leader."

One week before Sarah started kindergarten in September of 1979, Jim completed his psychology degree with honors. We moved from the campus of Trinity Western, and Jim continued working with One Way, in the new division of ministry he helped develop during his latter months in university.

The new ministry focused on young men who had suffered brain injuries as a result of car accidents. After they spent months and months in hospitals and physical rehabilitation, Jim worked with them to relearn social skills that they often practiced in our home. While he helped them adjust to their new reality and regain life focus, they also explored new skills to replace those that were no longer possible due to their injuries.

One young man who became our friend had made his living as a pianist. When he woke up from his accident, he found that he had lost most of the fingers on his right hand. His life as a performing pianist changed in a moment, but it took a very long time for him to adjust his thinking and redirect his musical gift to becoming a piano tuner. We were privileged to see him come to the Lord and take on a different role in life, before attending his wedding at the church where he met the love of his life.

Throughout the year, Grandma told us about the growing number of developers who wanted to buy her property, and we talked about the benefits that the sale could bring to Grandma. This had been her home, but it was primitive by many standards and lacked the comforts and conveniences we believed she needed and deserved. She agreed, and in September of 1980, Grandma sold the property where she and Grandpa Imerson had cleared the land and built their home. It had been hers for almost forty years and my home for most of my thirty years.

Grandma's diaries say that we started packing her belongings on January 5, 1981, but I know we spent many days throughout the fall of 1980 sorting through boxes and trunks and going down memory boulevard. On January 15, as we backed down the driveway and away from the house for the last time, Grandma was silent. I could only imagine the flood of emotions and memories that ran through her heart and mind. The house that she and Grandpa had built together was to be torn down to make room for condominiums. But knowing Grandma's adventurous spirit, I believe she looked ahead and gave thanks.

When Grandma and the moving van drove up to the large side-by-side duplex we had purchased together, our little family of four already had moved in the week before. It was wonderful to see Grandma so thrilled to be moving into a home with central heating, an amenity she never had in her previous home, and a mowed lawn with fruit trees. It was cold and raining on the outside but warm and sunny on the inside for all of us.

By the time Grandma decided to sell her home and the three of us agreed that we wanted to be together, she was adamant about what "living together" looked like. She didn't want a house where she would live in a basement suite. And if we were to move into a duplex, it had to be a side-by-side arrangement, not an up-and-down configuration. She valued her independence and made it clear that, at almost eighty-two years old, she was perfectly capable of looking after herself.

When we found a duplex that met all of our needs and desires, it had only one address, with the two sides differentiated by the numbers 9734A and 9734B. That wasn't enough individual identity for Grandma, so we applied to the city to give us two different addresses—even though the thirty-year-old, solidly constructed home had been recently rezoned as a single residence. Surprisingly, the city of Surrey granted our request. Grandma's home became 9736, and ours remained 9734. She was happy. She was home.

Grandma lived in her side of the duplex, and our little family lived in ours. But while we all went on with our own lives, we were often in each others' homes and did most things together.

When we moved into the duplex, there were two separate staircases that led up to small landings outside of our individual back doors. In order to take something to each other, we had to go down one flight of stairs, make our way across the lawn, and walk up the other flight of stairs. This was too much to expect of Grandma, so we devised a system of passing things like loaves of bread or cups of sugar on a six-foot-long board that was suspended between the rails of our two small landings.

It didn't take long before we removed the inside railings of the landings and placed a wide plank between them so we could walk back and forth to each other. Dangerous? Yes. Fun? It depends.

The summer after we moved in, we tore down the two small porches and staircases that had rotting support posts. In their place, we built a large deck that stretched across the back of the duplex and erected solid staircases on either end. The deck became a safe passageway for our many jaunts back and forth and a wonderful meeting and eating place in the summer.

## Personal Reflection

1. What happened in your life that you can look back on and say, "That was a miracle"?

2. When did you experience a desert place in your life? How did you find your way through it?

3. Recall a time when you experienced grace in your life. How can you demonstrate grace to your grandchildren?

4. Have you ever had a sense of restlessness in your life? What grounded you during that period of restlessness?

5. What would your grandma or grandpa say you were born to be or do?

6. If you moved into a living situation with your children and grandchildren, what would it be like?

# CHAPTER 28

# A Deadly Intruder

D URING THE YEAR and a half between when Jim finished his degree and we moved with Grandma to our duplex, Jim was approached by Vancouver Youth for Christ (YFC). They wanted him to head up the Youth Guidance division, working with families and kids on the streets of low-income areas. But the decision was not an easy one.

For almost a year, we repeatedly said "no." We were afraid of having to raise our own ongoing support and knew that leaving One Way would necessitate a lot of changes. After seven years, we had learned and experienced so much growth and felt a high level of loyalty to One Way and our friends. We were torn about leaving those who had enabled Jim to work in the ministry and receive a regular income while he finished his education.

The descriptive journal entries I wrote during that period of our lives give evidence of the turmoil we experienced. But God used that time of our lives to prepare us for the next steps of our journey.

Five months after moving into our duplex with Grandma, and after a lot of prayer and conversation with key people in our lives, we accepted the call to work with Youth for Christ, beginning in June of 1981. Thankfully, where we lived in our duplex was near the area Jim was going to work. A move was not required.

Ministering with YFC stretched Jim in a positive way. He learned to come alongside parents and teens alike and speak to churches and community groups about the work.

As for raising our own support and communicating regularly with our supporters, I'm not sure which of us was stretched the most. When our support didn't come in for a given month, I learned to make our shortages a game. I'd go through the kitchen cupboards and determine how many more meals I could get out of what we had. When we were near the end of my culinary creativity and what was available, Jim invariably came home with money that had come through for us that day.

I laugh about it now, but at the time, I remember almost being disappointed that money had come in. I rationalized that I was sure I could have made at least two or three more meals out of what we had—or it would have been fun to try. But God knew best. It wasn't about what I could do. It was about His provision for us and learning to trust Him—something I had watched Grandma do all through my growing-up years. And we never went hungry.

Grandma continued to mentor me through her actions. During our time with YFC, she became one of our faithful supporters. In addition to the personal extras she did for us along the way, she also made a monthly financial donation to our ministry. The support of people like my grandma and others on limited incomes gave me a deeper understanding of the Bible story about the widow's mite. I was humbled by the donations that were given in the spirit of cheerful, unconditional giving. What they gave may have seemed small compared to other donors who contributed larger amounts, but their gifts were huge. They gave sacrificially, faithfully, and lovingly. And I am forever grateful.

During the writing of this book, I read and reread Grandma's diary entries and struggled with feelings of guilt and remorse. Unfounded or not, I am even more acutely aware of what Grandma did for me and for us, and I wish I had told her more often how much I loved her, how much I appreciated who she was and what she did, and how much she taught me as her life intertwined so tightly with mine. I wish I could go back in time and give her the biggest hug and say the biggest "thank you" that anyone could give another person.

Last night I prayed, "God, I don't know how theologically sound this is—and I don't think it matters—but would You please give Grandma an extra special hug from me and tell her again how much I love and appreciate her?"

For the next three years, life was full for all of us. Grandma was busy with her many activities and gave leadership to some special initiatives. She also enjoyed a number of short trips with friends and a six-week vacation in 1982 to visit her remaining family in England, where she celebrated her eighty-third birthday.

While Grandma kept up with her busy schedule, Jim traveled and maintained his responsibilities at Youth for Christ. Meanwhile, I played drums with select music groups, traveled to speak at different women's events, and fulfilled various leadership roles. Our children also kept us busy with music, school, and church activities. And on occasion, Grandma and I attended retreats and worked together on some committees.

Every Tuesday was set aside for Grandma and me. After I dropped the children off at school, I took her to doctors' appointments, and we ran errands. We always stopped for lunch and did some shopping before picking the children up at the end of the day. According to Grandma, a not-to-be-missed event was $1.49 Day at Woodward's Department Store.

In July of 1984, Grandma's doctor saw something during her regular checkup and wanted her to undergo some tests. She, however, wanted to wait until we returned from the Youth for Christ International Conference in Hong Kong and our trip into mainland China. I reasoned with her that we would be gone for a full month and that if she had the tests done right away, the doctor would have the results by the time we came home. She agreed.

When we returned home from China on August 20, Grandma had received her test results and was scheduled for a scan of her liver and spleen on September 12. One month later, her spleen was removed, and on November 19, 1984, she received the ominous news that she had Hairy Cell Leukemia and Hodgkins Disease—two separate forms of cancer.

True to form, Grandma got right back to her commitments as soon as she could. The only things that interrupted her pace were the medical appointments she had to keep.

# CHAPTER 29

# Tables Turned Upside Down and Backwards

OVER THE NEXT months, Grandma and I saw more doctors, specialists, hospitals, and clinics. We sat in bright sterile rooms and sparse dim cubicles—sometimes in reflective silence and sometimes in thoughtful conversation. But we were always together.

In some of the rooms, I saw other courageous faces whose hushed sadness spoke of their own battles with cancer and the hope they clung to. When they were called to the next room for treatment, they made their way across the waiting room, and I'd hear Grandma whisper, "Poor soul."

As I waited, I assured myself that there was hope, that God was in control, and that the doctors knew more about cancer than they used to. Besides, they didn't know my Grandma. She was a fighter. She didn't give up.

To me, Grandma always had been a rock. Even when sadness filled her life, I saw her stand strong and firm. Nothing seemed to keep her down. "Where there's a will, there's a way," she'd often tell me. And I believed her.

On April 28, 1985, Grandma was rushed to hospital by ambulance but insisted they release her in time for the women's retreat she planned to attend in a month. She got her wish, and together we attended the retreat that her diary states was "good." It would be the last retreat or conference we'd attend together.

Despite the treatments, the disease took hold and wrestled to claim her body as its prize. I watched her go through surgery and experience the side effects of strong medications and chemotherapy. She became quieter, and I watched the fight drain from her face. I saw her once healthy body and active mind weaken as each day revealed one more reason to believe that our journey together was coming to an end.

One day in early July of 1985, I sat on the couch next to Grandma. Our quiet conversation turned to comfortable silence, and I heard the muffled sounds of my two children coming from the back deck. They were entertaining Grandma's two younger sisters, who had arrived a few days before for their three-month visit from England. The bi-annual trip had been scheduled before Grandma had received her cancer diagnosis eight months earlier. Though we lived right next door to Grandma and we had an intercom set up by her bed, I was grateful that my great aunts were staying in the house with her.

The sounds of my children's chatter from the back deck reminded me of how privileged I was to have a grandma who was such a major part of my life. I was grateful that she was very involved with my children, who loved her deeply.

As I watched Grandma stare quietly across the room toward the big picture window overlooking the thick holly hedge that grew along the front yard, I imagined what she was thinking. It had been four years since we bought this side-by-side duplex together, and now, in a few days, she would celebrate her eighty-sixth birthday—one more milestone to mark the way.

With my right arm around her shoulders, I ran my left hand along the emerald green upholstery of the couch. It had been twenty years since she purchased it, yet it still felt new. It was clear that Grandma always took care of her things.

Over the previous couple of weeks, what was once so effortless for Grandma had become a struggle for her—and order had become a stranger. Overdue notices for unpaid bills started to show up in the mail that I opened for her every morning. She didn't seem to know where she had left things. I kept finding bits of cash in unusual places throughout the house.

Grandma never had a lot of money, but since she was single and a widow most of her life, she learned to manage her affairs well. For as long as I can remember, she never purchased anything she couldn't pay for on the spot, and her bills were always paid on time. As I mentioned before, when she received the first and only credit card she applied for, she was careful to affirm that she only got it for identification purposes. She'd tell me, "If I use it to buy something, it's only to keep the card active. It's always paid before the statement comes in, so I don't have to pay interest." Then, as if she wanted to be sure I got the message about the pitfalls of credit, she'd add, "Never buy anything unless you have the money to pay for it. If it's important, it will wait." To my knowledge, Grandma never owed anyone anything.

Hesitant to break our quiet moment together, I slowly removed my arm from around her shoulder and turned to face her. I needed to talk to her about a delicate subject that I knew would be difficult for my proud and independent Grandma.

"Grandma, would you like me to do your banking later when I'm out? Or do you need me to mail any bill payments?" I asked.

No response. Instead, she continued looking straight ahead toward the window.

I persisted. "It's just that I've seen a couple of reminder notices come in the mail this week, so I thought you might like me to look after them for you."

I felt empty as I watched a defeated expression form on her face. I could see her struggle with emotions that were begging to spill out from her tired body. But, still, she said nothing.

"Grandma, why don't we look at what came in the mail? Then you can tell me what you'd like me to take care of for you."

Slowly, she reached over and picked up her heavy black-leather handbag from the floor and tried to open the metal clasp. Sheer determination won the battle, but soon that determination gave way to frustration as she fumbled with the contents of the bag.

When I was growing up, I was taught never to go into another woman's purse. It was personal. So I waited—not wanting to pry another piece of independence from her. Finally, I knew I needed to say something. "Grandma, why don't you let me help you?"

As our eyes met, her pride yielded, and with weakened hands, she let go of what she had always considered private.

Inside the black bag, I found a soft leather wallet with all her identification, a small change purse containing a number of coins, and a little plastic bag of Scotch Mints that were just like the ones she used to give me in church when I was a little girl. I also found a couple of pens, her 1985 pocket calendar, a notepad, her New Testament, the house keys, a nail clipper and file, a comb, and a number of envelopes with bits of money in each one.

The writing on the envelopes didn't look at all like Grandma's perfect penmanship. It was difficult to make out the words and numbers, but it became obvious to me that she had tried to set money aside to pay bills. While each envelope represented a different payment to be made, the figures written on the fronts of the envelopes didn't match the amounts of money inside.

As I thumbed through the pile on my lap, I felt a heavy weight push hard from inside my chest. My heart and mind were fighting against the path they were not yet ready to travel. In that moment, I realized we were taking the final steps towards an uninvited end. I knew it. And I could see that Grandma knew it too.

In the silence of that moment, we were introduced to our new reality. A thoughtless and malignant intruder had laid claim to this adventurous and giving woman who had been my friend, my mentor—my grandma. And now she, who always had been strong and dependable, had become weakened and dependent.

We looked into each other's faces, and I saw tears fill her eyes. She leaned towards me and did something I never had seen her do before. She laid her head on my shoulder and cried. After a brief moment, she whispered, "Oh, Ann, what am I going to do?"

I couldn't speak. Tenderly, I reached up to stroke her soft, thin, white hair and hold her close. She had always been there for me—to comfort me when my world was less than perfect, to encourage me when life was hard, and to cradle me in her arms when I needed to feel safe. But now it was different. As she lay on my shoulder, I could sense that she now needed what she had so freely and unconditionally given to me. The tables had turned—upside down and backwards.

# CHAPTER 30

# Commitment at a Price

A T GRANDMA'S REQUEST, a couple of days later, we celebrated her eighty-sixth birthday with little fanfare. Normally, we would have gone to a local restaurant and talked about what was going on in our lives while we enjoyed a chicken or seafood entrée with all the trimmings. After the main course, we'd choose a decadent dessert to go with fresh coffee. Grandma would open the cards and gifts we brought, being careful not to tear the wrapping paper.

This year, however, only an intimate group of nine gathered in our home to honor her and the day of her birth, July 10, 1899. Along with Grandma and me, there were Grandma's two sisters, Hilda and Doris; Grandma's friend Hilda; my sister, Pat; our two children, Sarah and James; and Jim.

Grandma had worked her way up to head cook of two small hotels in London, England, when she was young. She was an excellent cook and appreciated good food. But on this special day, I watched as she struggled to take a few bites from the Black Forest cake, which was one of her favorites. I still don't know how we ever thought she had the energy to blow out so many candles. Yet she managed a smile when we placed the large dessert in front of her, and then she good-naturedly tried to blow out the miniature flames that covered the top of it.

I wish we had never taken the photos we took that day, and I seldom look at them even today. They show a tired and strained face with a forced, polite smile, which was so unlike the grandma I knew and want to remember. I can't help but imagine that she was trying her best for us and saying to herself, "Where there's a will, there's a way. I can do this."

One week later, on July 18, the doctor insisted that Grandma be admitted to the hospital, where they could provide the necessary pain relief on a regular basis. At first she was in a semi-private room, but later she was moved to a different ward and a private room. I was told that when terminally ill patients were near the end of life, the staff preferred to put them in their own rooms, for dignity's sake. In a short while, I would come to appreciate fully their wisdom and thoughtfulness.

I spent the next couple of days with Grandma, taking only short breaks when a friend or member of the family came to visit. Grandma had been ill for less than a year, but until the middle of June, she continued her responsibilities at church and commitments to her family and friends. One friend later said at her memorial, "We knew she hadn't been feeling well, but we had no idea she was so sick. She didn't let on how sick she really was."

I had never heard Grandma complain about decisions she'd made, even though I thought that she probably felt like it at times. I couldn't remember a time when she hadn't followed through on a commitment she'd made—no matter how bad she felt at the time.

Being careful not to wake her, I got up from the chair by her hospital bed. After stretching my legs and arms, I took a few steps toward the window to look at a collage of photos I'd arranged in a frame on the window sill. My mind raced with scenes of the things we'd shared, and I wondered what she thought about now as she lay in the hospital.

*What about those long Tuesday bus rides, Grandma? Do you think about the family and friends you left behind to move to the strange new world of Canada? Do you reminisce about my grandpa—the man you had never met but whom you sailed across the ocean to marry? Do you wonder if you did the right thing by not going back to England when you were widowed five years later? Do you have second thoughts about choosing to raise your four-year-old daughter here by yourself? I remember you saying, "I made my choice when I left, so I wasn't about to go running home to Mom and Dad and be a burden to them when things got tough." But I'm sure that, at times, it was sheer will that kept you here.*

*On those long bus trips, did you think happy thoughts about people like Flora's mother, Rose, who was there when you needed a friend? It must have been hard when she died. Is that why you kept taking that long trip until you were way past seventy years old? Were you repaying an old friend when you cleaned house for her husband and daughter—Uncle Jack and Aunt Flora?*

I had no idea how difficult it must have been for Grandma. At fifty-one years of age, after being widowed a second time, she had taken on the all-consuming task of caring for me, a two-month-old baby, while still raising her fourteen-year-old step-grandson who was living with her. She provided for us by cleaning people's houses, doing their ironing, tending their gardens, and finding other odd jobs, like mending fishing nets and painting houses. Her example taught me to honor my commitments. Now I wanted to remind her how much I loved her and appreciated all she had done for me.

## PERSONAL REFLECTION

1. What happened in your life that turned it upside down and backwards?

2. Who do you know that is struggling and may need someone to come alongside them? What could you do that would make a difference to them?

3. If you were to receive news that you had an incurable disease, what would your children and grandchildren remember about your response to it?

4. Recall a special birthday celebration with one or both of your grandparents. What made it special?

5. As a grandparent, how can you show love and appreciation to your grandchildren? How would you like your grandchildren to show love and appreciation to you?

# CHAPTER 31

# Responsibility Is a Two-Edged Sword

B EFORE MY GREAT aunts Hilda and Doris had arrived from England in June, Grandma and I had talked about Jim and me taking them with our children to Three Hills, Alberta, for our church national conference at the end of July. I had responsibilities there as National President of Women's Ministries of Canada and was scheduled to leave on July 21. But three days before we were to leave, Grandma was admitted to the hospital.

Six years had passed since Grandma encouraged me to work with the women of our church, followed by district leadership. Now I was ending my first year of a three-year term as President of the National Board. The conference also marked the end of the first full year since the inception of Women's Ministries of Canada. This was an important milestone for me and for the women involved.

But things had changed since that conversation a couple of months before. With the turn of events in Grandma's life and her admission to the hospital, I spent every day with her and felt torn about leaving her to attend the conference. When she slept, I worked on details for the conference and the talks I was expected to give. While at home in the early mornings and late evenings, I met with members of my team and made phone calls in the midst of caring for my family.

The morning after Grandma was admitted to the hospital, I came in early and found her wearing what appeared to be a straight jacket and sitting in a chair. I was horrified and demanded to know why she was being treated this way. After all, she wasn't mentally unbalanced.

Calmly, the nurse explained that it was because she had tried to get up by herself. They had caught her just before she fell.

I realized that this was one time when Grandma's independence was not helping her. She was so accustomed to doing for herself that she never thought twice about getting up on her own. The problem now was that she had become weak and wasn't very clearheaded due to the medication.

With me sitting close by, the nurse untied Grandma, and she and I sat quietly until I interrupted the silence. "Want to play a game of Crib, Grandma?" I asked.

"We could," she replied softly.

We had played Cribbage for hours in the past, and she was a master. As her sickness progressed, I had decided that keeping up with the game might help to keep her alert. Over the years, she had often told me that she never wanted to lose her mental capacity. But on this day, as I watched her slowly pick up each card and struggle to think through the counting and which card to play next, I could see she wasn't enjoying the game.

"Grandma, you look like you're getting tired. Would you like to finish the game later?" I asked.

"That would be good," she replied. "I am feeling a bit tired."

We never did get back to that game. It was the last time we ever played Cribbage together.

The next morning, I came into Grandma's hospital room and saw her lying down with each wrist tied to the side rails of the bed. Before waking her, I went to the nurse and asked what was going on. Again, I learned that she had tried to get out of bed by herself. "It's for her own safety that we restrained her," explained the nurse.

As I walked back to her bed, she opened her eyes, and seeing it was me, she pleaded, "Ann, please help me get up."

"I can't, Grandma," I choked.

"But if you don't help me out of this bed, I will never get up again. Ann, please help me out of bed."

When the nurse came in to free her from the restraints, my heart cried in silence as I tried to explain why they had tied her hands and why she couldn't get out of bed without someone there.

To this day, I regret not helping her up. Even though I know it's not true, I still struggle with the "maybe." Maybe if I had helped her up, she would have lived longer. Maybe she thought I had given up on her and that there was no more hope. Maybe . . . Maybe . . . Maybe . . .

From that day on, she never again got out of bed.

Today, I know deep down that the "maybes" aren't true, but I still feel the emotion when I think of that incident. Grandma was a courageous woman who met life's challenges head on and didn't back down. But on that day, she had no choice. Others were choosing for her. Did we choose well?

The day after she begged me to help her out of bed, we were scheduled to leave for the conference, but we delayed our departure by one day. I didn't want to leave, but as Grandma and I talked briefly about it, we both knew I had to follow through on my commitment.

I assured her that I'd be back in a week, as soon as my responsibilities were over, and that my sister would be in to see her every day. I also told her about a list of friends and family I had arranged to sit with her every day that I was gone. And I showed her the visitor sign-in paper I was leaving beside her bed for people to sign so she and I could talk about who had been in to see her while I was away.

Before kissing her good-bye, I assured her that I would call my sister twice a day to see how she was doing and that I would drop everything and come home right away if needed.

On July 22, at 6:00 A.M., Jim and I loaded up our VW bus with our two children, my two great aunts, and luggage for all of us, and we headed for Three Hills, Alberta. All the way there and during the conference, I wanted to turn around and go back to Grandma. Yet I was pulled by a sense of responsibility to my commitments, which Grandma had encouraged and pointed me toward all my life. While I hated leaving her, I also knew that I was doing exactly what she had taught me.

Faithfully, I called twice a day for updates, until the time finally came to head home. Again, we all piled into our VW bus and started driving west toward the mountains. When we reached the halfway mark on the road home, we stopped for the night in Revelstoke, British Columbia, and checked into a hotel. When I called my sister, Pat, she sounded anxious and told me that she'd been waiting for my call. "You have to come right away," she said, "Grandma is not doing well."

I hung up the phone and told Jim and my aunts what was happening and that we had to leave right away. Their response wasn't what I expected at all.

"Ann, we've been driving a long time. The children are already asleep, and we're all tired. We should get some rest and leave in the morning."

But I was determined. There was no way I was going to lie around when my grandma needed me. "OK. I'll take the bus. It will get me there in the morning, and you can all come after you've slept."

They also were determined. "No, you need to sleep too. If we all go to bed now, we can get up early and be there before the bus."

Grudgingly, I gave in. We agreed that we'd get up at 4:00 in the morning and drive straight through. I don't think I slept much that night, but true to their word, we headed out on time. I now know that when they made me wait until morning, they were being wise and thinking about what lay ahead in the days to come.

By 9:00 A.M., we were almost home. When we pulled up to the hospital, I got out of the van and said a quick "good-bye" over my shoulder, leaving Jim to drive the family home and unload the car. I ran to the big glass entrance doors of the hospital, rushed down the hallway, got into the elevator, and pushed the button for Grandma's floor. The ride seemed to take forever, as people got on and off at every floor on the way up to the fifth floor. All I could think of was getting up to Grandma's room as fast as I could.

Finally, the elevator stopped at my destination, and the doors opened. I stepped out and turned left toward the hall that led to her room. As I rounded the next corner, I saw a group of people gathered in the middle of the hallway. When I got closer to them, I saw that family members were standing outside Grandma's room.

*Oh, no. I'm too late*, I thought as I felt my heart jump and a sick feeling overcome me.

When I reached the somber crowd, I didn't want anyone to touch me. One of my brothers motioned to the room and said, "Pat and Mom are inside with Grandma."

Still not sure what to expect, I took a deep breath and stepped into the room.

# CHAPTER 32

# That's My Girl

AS I WALKED toward Grandma's hospital bed, my sister leaned over, and I heard her say, "Grandma, Ann's here." Grandma turned her head to face me, and a gentle but weak smile came over her face. I took her soft warm hand in my left hand, cupped her face in my right hand, and bent down to kiss her.

Softly, but loud enough for all to hear, she said, "That's my girl. Everything's OK now."

Everyone looked at each other with shocked expressions on their faces. "Those are the first words any of us have heard her speak since you left a week ago," they proclaimed.

To me, those days I was away seemed like an eternity.

Grandma showed obvious signs of tiredness as the family members who had been waiting in the hallway trickled into the room. She managed a weak smile as each one bent over to kiss her good-bye and left the room as quietly as they had arrived. When only my sister, mom, and Grandma's close friend Ivy Anhorn were left in the room with me, we stood with my sister and me on either side of her bed and Mom and Ivy at her feet.

After a few quiet moments, Mom moved to the side of the bed where my sister stood. When Grandma saw her coming closer and Mom began to say "good-bye," Grandma turned away from her and toward me.

Without recognition or affirmation from my grandma, Mom backed away and slowly walked out of the room. She never returned.

As I think back to that scene, I feel hurt for my mom and sad for my grandma. Over the previous forty years, their relationship had been anything but a wonderful, loving mother-daughter affair. I had witnessed some of the paralyzing words and silences that had taken place, and I knew about some of the hurtful things that had occurred over the years. Was Grandma wrong? Was Mom wrong? Were they both wrong? Was anyone wrong? Could any of it be so bad that in the last days and hours of a person's life forgiveness and reconciliation could not be a reality? What would it take to heal the gaping and infected wounds?

So much of the grandma I knew, the life she had lived, and the principles she had taught me conflicted with the obvious rejection of her only child on that day. It's a scene that haunted me for a long time. I wondered if the physical struggle Grandma experienced in her final two weeks on this earth was compounded by a raging battle going on inside of her—a battle between the truth of what she knew and believed and the reality of her painful experiences.

At one point in Grandma's final hours, when she no longer was able to communicate verbally, it seemed that a wave of peace came over her. Was it a sign that she finally had come to a place of forgiveness and now was free of the anger, hurt, and betrayal she seemed to hang on to for many years? I don't know.

But this I do know: Grandma faced challenge after challenge with the attitude that "this is the way things are, so we'll make the best of it." But her outward appearance of contentment and the servant's heart that she so willingly shared with others was shadowed by the reality that forgiveness, reconciliation, and healing evaded her in her relationship with her daughter.

It didn't take long for my family or the nurses to realize that I wasn't moving from Grandma's hospital room. Every morning when the doctors came in, I was there. When nurses came in to tend to her needs or check on her morphine drip, I was there. When friends or family came to visit, I was there. When Grandma closed her eyes, I was there. And when she opened them, she looked at me, smiled, and squeezed my hand. I knew she wanted me there. I wasn't about to leave.

After being away for the week-long conference, it was wonderful to be with her again—to hold her hand, stroke her forehead, and speak softly with her. We truly had missed each other. From that day on, we were together day and night.

The nurses never gave me a bad time about being at the hospital all the time. Instead, they voiced their concern that I needed to sleep and brought me a blanket and pillow to stay warm while I sat in the upright, high-backed chair. When they had time to stop for a moment, we chatted while Grandma slept. After a week passed, they brought a cot with bedding into her private room so that I at least could lie down at night.

But sleep became very difficult for me as Grandma's pain increased. When the male nurses came to turn her every two or three hours, they began asking me to leave the room while they did it. I don't know what was worse—being in the room as she screamed in pain when they moved her or standing outside her room as she screamed in pain when they moved her. Either way, I felt helpless to do anything about what was happening to my grandma.

Each day, her breathing became more labored. Every breath was an effort, and it got to the point where her struggle could be heard by other patients and by visitors down the hallway.

At one point, her doctor, who also had been my doctor since I was a girl of nine, came into the room and, with compassion in his voice, said, "Ann, there's something we need to talk about, and I need you to make a decision." He then proceeded to tell me that there was nothing more they could do for Grandma except to try and keep her comfortable. His tenderness toward my grandma showed in his tearful eyes and compassionate voice as he said, "Ann, your grandma has a very strong heart, and right now, if it wasn't for that strong heart, she would be gone." He went on to say that they needed to know whether or not they should resuscitate her when she stopped breathing.

Tears welled up in my eyes as I asked him what I should do, and he handed me a form to sign. I trusted him. He had been our doctor since he started practicing medicine, and Grandma spoke of him with great respect. He almost felt like part of the family.

"This is a Do Not Resuscitate or DNR form, Ann. You need to read it over carefully and sign it if you want Grandma to go when she's ready to go. But if she stops breathing and you want us to bring her back, don't sign it. Just remember that she's ready to go."

I knew what I needed to do—what Grandma would want me to do. I had watched her world change drastically in less than a year as she struggled against two cancers at one time. At that time, the medical treatment for one of the cancers seemed to cause the other cancer to flare up, and vice versa. Now she was so tired. She didn't have the strength to speak, and morphine was trying to keep up with the pain that was growing stronger each day. As I stood there by the door and listened to her fight for each and every breath, I took a pen and signed the DNR.

The last week was the hardest. Each day, I sat and tried to write or read. Sometimes I'd read out loud, and other times I'd lean over and rest my head on the bed beside Grandma.

One day, different nurses expressed concern about Grandma's wedding ring that was getting tighter on her finger. A few days earlier, they had wanted to remove it with lotion, but I had refused. I reasoned that Grandma's wedding ring had never left her finger and that if we removed it, she might sense that we had given up on her and that it would mean the end.

Finally, I gave in when they explained that the ring was beginning to constrict the blood flow in her swelling hand. When two male nurses came into her room, cut the ring off her finger, reached across her bed, and dropped two pieces of gold into my hand, I fought to hold back the emotion that welled up inside of me.

On another occasion, I recall a nurse quietly checking on Grandma. Lifting my head from Grandma's bed, I nodded and said, "Thank you."

"You're welcome, dear. Are you OK? You know, you really should get some proper rest."

"I know. But I'm fine, thank you. Did you see these photos?" I asked, pointing towards the window sill.

"Yes, some of us were commenting on them. She looks like she was quite a lady."

"Yes, she *is*," I corrected.

"You're right, dear. She is."

As she turned to leave the room, she stopped, looked back, and said, "We try not to get attached to our patients, but some of us have really grown fond of your grandma."

With that, she smiled and quickly left the room.

"See, Grandma," I whispered, "even lying here, you're making a difference."

When friends or family came to visit, they insisted that since they were there, I could take a break for a few minutes. So, under pressure, I'd go to the visitor's lounge or walk up and down the hall. The only time I left the floor was when I periodically walked to my home a block away to take a quick shower before doing a fast walk back to Grandma's side.

As the week wore on and Grandma's breathing became louder and more labored, the nurses told me they felt bad that they couldn't tell me how long Grandma could go on in that state, and they were sorry they couldn't do more for her.

On August 12, 1985, Grandma's and my friend Eileen Enarson was our only visitor. When she left at the end of visiting hours in the evening, one of the nurses came into the room to check on Grandma. When the nurse started to leave, I looked up and said, "Thank you for what you're doing for my grandma."

She stopped, looked in my direction, and stepped toward me. "Ann, we can't say when someone is going to pass away, but," she whispered, "I don't think you should be alone tonight. I think you should have someone here with you."

When she left the room, I looked at Grandma's face and stroked her soft, swollen hand. The reality that these were probably our final hours together was setting in. I didn't even think about who to call—my husband, my closest friend, my sister, my great aunts, my . . . My head was spinning, my body was shaking, and my heart was crying.

Quietly, I stood up, walked to the pay phone just outside of Grandma's room, and called Eileen. She just had arrived home and said she'd come to the hospital right away.

When she walked into the room, I had my head down by Grandma and was reciting her favorite Psalm—Psalm 23. "The Lord is my shepherd. I shall not want . . ."

Eileen and I didn't have to say a word to each other. She simply sat down on a chair beside me, put her arm around my shoulders, and began singing softly with her beautiful, angelic voice.

After a few minutes, she told me that I needed sleep and that while I rested only a couple of feet away on the cot, she would sit by Grandma. I argued that I wouldn't leave her side, but Eileen insisted. She had walked this road before.

Throughout the night, we took turns on the cot while each breath forced another bit of life into Grandma's body.

Just before six o'clock on the morning of Tuesday, August 13, 1985, I jumped from the cot when Grandma's breathing suddenly changed. Between each breath there were long pauses, and I could feel her wrist beating a shallow pulse. During the long waits for another breath, I'd hear myself coax her on to take another.

When she took her last gasp and there were no more breaths left to mix with my tears, Eileen whispered, "I'm going to go get the nurse, Ann."

"No, not yet," I choked.

All was quiet—no noise, no talking, no breathing, no gasping—just quiet tears—until Eileen broke the silence.

"Ann, I really need to go get the nurse now," she whispered again.

I didn't want anyone to come between me and my grandma, but I knew Eileen was right, so I gave a slight nod.

When she walked out of the room, all I heard were my own muffled sobs. I gazed down at Grandma lying peaceful and still. No more struggle. No more pain. No more breath. I wanted to bend over and kiss her, but I told myself that when I did that, it would be final—the end. She would be gone. If I just could hold off a little longer, we could be together for a few more minutes—at least until Eileen came back with the nurse.

As I stood there with her hand in mine and stroked her soft, white hair, I had the overwhelming sense that I was not alone—that Grandma was still in the room. Her presence was there, and we were having our last moments together in the silence. I felt her arms wrapped around me, holding me close, comforting and encouraging me. She knew how I felt because, years before, she had been here in my place, grieving over the loss of someone she loved.

In the past, we had been there for each other through good and bad. We loved each other through it all. Now, in this moment, we shared something very special that only Grandma and I could share together.

Then, as if on cue, I leaned over, held Grandma close, and kissed her softly. It was time.

"Bye, Grandma. I love you. I'll see you later," I whispered.

And she was gone.

# CHAPTER 33

# Generation Upon Generation

A LIFETIME HAS PASSED since Grandma and I said "good-bye" and she went to heaven. Our children, Sarah and James, were only ten and nine years old at the time. And me? I just had turned thirty-five, but I felt like my life was over. In some ways, it was—as I knew it.

It took me a year even to begin to go through Grandma's possessions, and some of them are still in our home. Every time I walked into her side of our duplex, my senses of smell and touch and hearing came alive. It was as if she was still there and I could hear her call from the next room.

Fifteen years after she passed away, we sold the duplex, and after everyone else was gone, I took a final stroll around the property. As I said "good-bye" one more time, it was as if Grandma and I were walking together. In my mind's eye, I could see her inspect the four fruit trees and hear her estimate how much fruit we might get that year—if the crows stayed away. When I looked up to the back deck, I could see her leaning against the rail to watch me work in the garden as she offered words of encouragement and instruction. That stroll represented the end of another chapter in the book that Grandma and I had written together. And life went on.

Today, memories and photos still spark emotions that rise to the surface. I still miss the talks she and I enjoyed and the wisdom and practical advice she gave. Now, as a grandma myself, I try to model what she and I had together by nurturing the relationships that I share with my grandchildren, Victoria, Anthony, Calista, and Lucas.

Writing about Grandma's and my life together has been one of the hardest things I've ever done. What started out as a book to inspire and encourage grandmas in the vital role they play also turned out to be a healing process that I needed to experience. It has shown me the miracle of God's grace and His faithfulness throughout our personal challenges, victories, failures, and shortcomings. I believe that it has helped me to realize even more how important my role really is as a mom and grandma.

As the years have passed, I've realized that Grandma's life isn't really over. Oh, it's over physically, but who she was is not over. She lives on in me, in my children whom she knew and loved very much, and in other members of our extended family who knew her. Her life lives on through the life skills she taught, the character she demonstrated, and the eternal values she believed and modeled. She also lives on in who my grandchildren are becoming, because her life left a permanent fingerprint on my life and on their parents' lives. But that's not the end. My grandchildren too will leave a mark on more generations to come.

*Wow!* The difference one life makes. The difference we each will make. It's the miracle of life that God created.

When my granddaughter Victoria wasn't yet three years old, she sat on my lap, pointed to the lone portrait on the table beside us, and asked, "Who's that, Grandma?"

I replied, "That's your great-great grandma. That's Grandma's Grandma."

It was then that this book was conceived, though it took more than ten years to complete. I hope that through these pages, a toddler's innocent question has been answered.

I trust that the unwavering spirit of my grandma is now more real to you—that you have a deeper understanding of the mark one grandma can leave and the difference it can continue to make as it weaves from generation to generation to generation. May you, and others who read these pages, be inspired and encouraged by the heart of a grandma's life and love and the difference it made and continues to make.

When you sit with a child on your lap, may you marvel at what God has done in the lives of those who went before you and left a mark on your life. May the child who sits with you be drawn to the beautiful creation that is you.

This book began with a letter to a toddler. Today, she and her brother and cousins are teenagers and I am bringing the expanded version of this book to a close. Yet the story is not finished. When we all get to heaven, I look forward to standing face-to-face with my grandma and to the thrill of introducing Victoria, Anthony, Lucas, and Calista to their great-great grandma—my grandma whose life mingled with mine to mold me into the grandma that I am for them.

On August 13, 1985, I felt like my life was over. But it really was only another beginning—the beginning of endless beginnings . . . a story with no end.

## Personal Reflection

1. When has a sense of responsibility pulled you away from where your heart wanted to be?

2. What regret or "maybe" or "if only" do you need to let go of?

3. As you reflect on your grandparents, what are you most thankful for?

4. What words of wisdom did you receive from your grandparents that have stayed with you throughout your life?

5. What words of wisdom would you like your grandchildren to remember hearing from you?

# Contact Information